At the age of sixty, Cory Taylor is dying of melanoma-related brain cancer. Her illness is no longer treatable: she now weighs less than her neighbor's retriever. As her body weakens, she details the experience—the vulnerability and strength, the courage and humility, the anger and acceptance—of knowing she will soon die.

Written in the space of a few weeks, in a tremendous creative surge, this powerful and beautifully written memoir is a clear-eyed account of what dying teaches: Taylor describes the tangle of her feelings, remembers the lives and deaths of her parents, and examines why she would like to be able to choose the circumstances of her death.

Cory Taylor's last words offer a vocabulary for readers to speak about the most difficult thing any of us will face. And while *Dying: A Memoir* is a deeply affecting meditation on death, it is also a funny and wise tribute to life.

DYING

· a memoir ·

Cory Taylor

Tin House Books
Portland, Oregon & Brooklyn, New York

Published by Tin House Books, Portland, Oregon, and Brooklyn, New York

Distributed by W. W. Norton & Company

Library of Congress Cataloging-in-Publication Data is available.

ISBN: 978-1-941040-70-6

First US Edition 2017
Printed in the USA
Interior design by Diane Chonette

www.tinhouse.com

To Shin

I

COLD FEET

About two years ago I bought a euthanasia drug online from China. You can get it that way, or you can travel to Mexico or Peru and buy it over the counter from a vet. Apparently you just say you need to put down a sick horse and they'll sell you as much as you want. Then you either drink it in your Lima hotel room, and let your family deal with the details of shipping your remains home, or you smuggle it back in your luggage for later use. I wasn't intending to use mine straightaway, and I wasn't fit to travel all the way to South America, so I chose the China option.

My Chinese drug comes in powdered form. I keep it in a vacuum-sealed bag in a safe and secret place, along with a suicide note. I wrote the note over a year ago, a few days before I was due to have brain surgery. I had melanoma in the part of my brain that controls the movement of my limbs on the right side—incurable, no guarantee that the cancer wouldn't return after the surgery. By then I had deposits of melanoma elsewhere too, in my right lung, under the skin on my right arm, a big one just below my liver, another pressing on my urethra, which had necessitated the insertion in 2011 of a plastic stent to keep my right kidney functioning.

I had been first diagnosed in 2005, just before my fiftieth birthday, after a biopsy on a mole excised from the back of my right knee came back positive as a stage-four melanoma. Since then the progress of my disease had been mercifully slow. It was three years before it showed up in my pelvic lymph nodes and another couple of years before it began to spread to other parts of my body. I had two rounds of surgery, from which I recovered well, and in between I suffered no debilitating symptoms. In that time I managed to keep my illness a secret from all but my closest friends. Only my husband, Shin, knew the whole story, because he'd accompanied me to my regular scans and specialist appointments. But I had kept the details from our two teenage sons, trying, I suppose, to protect them from pain, because that was my job as their mother. Then, in late December 2014, a seizure left me temporarily helpless as a baby and I could no longer deny the obvious.

So we convened a family meeting in our home in inner-city Brisbane—Shin, our younger son, Dan, his girlfriend, Linda, our older son, Nat, and his wife, Asako, who dropped everything and flew home from Kyoto, where they'd been living for two years. Over the next few days, I took them through all the paperwork they'd need to access if the worst happened: my will, their Powers of Attorney, my bank accounts, tax, superannuation. It helped me to feel that I was putting my house in order, and I think it helped them because it made them feel useful. I even revealed my interest in euthanasia drugs and evasively said they were on my wish list for Christmas. I called it my Marilyn Monroe gift pack.

"If it was good enough for her, it's good enough for me," I said. "Even if I never use it, just knowing it's there would give me a sense of control."

And, to the extent that they didn't object, I think they understood.

My suicide note was by way of an apology. "I'm sorry," I wrote. "Please forgive me, but if I wake up from the surgery badly impaired, unable to walk, entirely dependent on other people to care for me, I'd prefer to end my own life." I also repeated what I'd told them a hundred times to their faces: how much I loved them all, and how much joy they had brought me. Thank you, I told them. Talk to me when I'm gone, and I'll be listening. I wasn't sure that was true, but it was as metaphysical as I was ever going to get, and it did make a kind of sense at the time, given that I was already writing to the living from the point of view of the dead.

As it happened, I came through the surgery, not entirely unimpaired, but not too badly off. The tumour in my brain was successfully removed. My right foot will never fully recover its strength, so I limp, but I have normal movement in the rest of my right side. And, over a year after the operation, I'm still here. Nevertheless, my situation remains dire. There is no cure for melanoma. A few drugs are being trialled, with varying results. I've been involved in three drug trials, and I can't say for certain whether any of them slowed the disease. All I do know is that, despite my oncologist's best efforts, I eventually ran out of treatment options. It was then that I became certain I was coming to the end. I didn't know when, or exactly how, I was going to die, but I knew I wasn't going to make it much beyond my sixtieth birthday.

With my health deteriorating steadily, I started to focus on the question of suicide like never before. After all, in a first for me, I'd gone to the extent of breaking the law and risking prosecution, in order to obtain the means. My stash calls to me day and night, like an illicit lover. Let me take you away from all this, it whispers. My drug would go straight to the sleep centre of the brain in the time it takes to finish a sentence. What could be easier than to swallow a fatal dose and never wake up again? Surely that would be preferable to the alternative, which is a lingering and gruesome demise?

And yet I hesitate, because what appears to be a clear-cut solution is anything but. Firstly, there are the practicalities of my taking such a course of action. As the law stands in Australia, I would have to take my drug alone, so as not to implicate anyone else in my death. Even though suicide is not a crime, assisting a person to suicide is illegal and is punishable by a lengthy jail term. Secondly, there are the emotional repercussions for others should I do the deed, be it in a hotel room somewhere, or on a lonely bush track. I ask myself if I have the right to traumatise some hotel cleaner, or some bushwalker, unfortunate enough to discover my corpse. Of paramount concern to me are the repercussions for Shin and the boys of my taking my own life, for as much as I've tried to prepare them for the possibility that I might, I know the reality would shake them to the core. It worries me, for instance, that my death certificate would read "suicide" as cause of death, with everything that the term implies these days: mental angst, hopelessness, weakness, the lingering whiff of criminality—a far cry from, say, the Japanese tradition of seppuku, or suicide for honour's sake. The fact that cancer was actually my killer would be lost to posterity, as would the fact that I am not, by any fair measure, mad.

Faced with all of these obstacles, I contemplate my bleak future with as much courage as I can muster. I'm lucky to have found an excellent palliative care specialist and an exceptional home nursing service, so, along with my family and friends, I have as much support as I could wish for. If I were, however, to express a wish to end my own life, none of that support would be legally available to me. I would be strictly on my own. Our laws, unlike those in countries such as Belgium and the Netherlands, continue to prohibit any form of assisted dying for people in my situation. It occurs to me to ask why. I wonder, for instance, if our laws reflect some deep aversion amongst medical professionals here towards the idea of relinquishing control of the dying process into the hands of the patient. I wonder if this aversion might stem from a more general belief in the medical profession that death represents a form of failure. And I wonder if this belief hasn't seeped out into the wider world in the form of an aversion to the subject of death per se, as if the stark facts of mortality can be banished from our consciousness altogether.

Surely there couldn't be a more futile exercise, for if cancer teaches you one thing, it is that we are dying in our droves, all the time. Just go into the oncology department of any major hospital and sit in the packed waiting room. All around you are people dying. See most of them on the street, and you'd never know it, but here they are lined up, waiting for the latest results of their scans, to discover if they've beaten the odds this month. It's a shocking sight if you're unused to it. I was as under-prepared as anyone could be. It was as if I had stumbled out of a land of make-believe into the realm of the real.

That is why I started writing this book. Things are not as they should be. For so many of us, death has become the unmentionable thing, a monstrous silence. But this is no help to the dying, who are probably lonelier now than they've ever been. At least that is how it feels to me.

o

I had never seen anybody die. Until my mother became demented I had never even seen anyone gravely ill. My mother's decline was slow at first, and then very fast. Towards the end she was barely recognisable as the mother I had so loved and admired. I was out of the country when she finally died, but I was there in the months preceding her death and I saw the ravages she suffered, the pain and humiliation, the loss of independence and reason.

She was in a nursing home when she died, a place of such unremitting despair it was a test of my willpower just to walk through the front door. The last time I saw her, I stood helplessly by while she had her arse wiped clean by a young Japanese nurse. My mother was clinging on to a bathroom basin with all of her meagre strength, while the nurse applied a fresh nappy to her withered behind. The look in my mother's eyes as she turned and saw me watching reminded me of an animal in unspeakable torment. At that moment I wished for death to take her quickly, to stop the torture that had become her daily life. But still it went on, for a dozen more months, her body persisting while her mind had long since vacated the premises. I could not think of anything more cruel and unnecessary. I knew I had cancer by then, and a part of me was grateful. At least I would be spared a death like my mother's, I reasoned. That was something to celebrate.

It was my mother who introduced me to the debate around assisted dying. She first came across the voluntary euthanasia movement, as it was then known, some time in her sixties, and I knew it was a cause she continued to support, because she made a point of telling me. Back then I took far less notice than I should have. My mother was asking me for help, but it wasn't clear what kind of help she wanted. Perhaps just a bit of encouragement to look into the problem more closely, to obtain the necessary means if it came to that. I wasn't very receptive. In those days there was nothing wrong with my mother, or with me, so her arguments in support of the concept of assisted dying were purely academic. Of course, by the time they were real and urgent, my mother had left it too late to put theory into practice, and her mind had lost its edge, so that even the most well-meaning doctor in the world could not have helped her, despite her years of devotion to the cause.

I wasn't there when my father died either, also in a nursing home, and also from complications arising from dementia. My parents had divorced some thirty-five years previously and I had subsequently become estranged from my father. But one of my abiding memories of him is his fantasy solution to the indignities of old age. He told us—me, my mother, and my older siblings—that he planned to sail out into the Pacific Ocean and drown himself. He repeatedly baulked at the first hurdle, however, by never obtaining a boat. He would read boat magazines and circle the For Sale ads in them. He would drive long distances to look over boats he liked the sound of, but he would always find a reason not to buy. Money was short, or he didn't want to sail alone. At one point, he even asked my mother to buy a half share and to crew for him, an offer she declined. Maybe she should have taken him up on it. Maybe they should have sailed off into the sunset never to return; instead they lived on and died badly.

No doubt my horror at how my parents ended their days influenced me to look into ways I might improve things when it came to my turn. With this in mind, soon after I was diagnosed with cancer, I followed my mother's lead and joined Exit International, wanting to get up to speed on the latest developments in the assisted dying field. I also joined Dignitas in Switzerland, where it is legal for foreigners to obtain assistance to die, provided they are suffering from a terminal illness. This was an information-gathering exercise to explore the choices available to me, other than those offered by my doctors. I don't wish to disparage the doctors who have cared for me over time. Individually they've been extraordinary, and of course I owe them a debt of gratitude. Apart from the

palliative care specialists I've spoken to, however, none of
my doctors ever raised the subject of death with me, a fact
I still find mystifying.

So another motive for joining Exit was to find a forum
for simply broaching the topic, challenging the taboo that
I felt was preventing my doctors from speaking openly to
me about something so pertinent. Despite the ubiquity of
death, it seems strange that there are so few opportunities
to publicly discuss dying. Exit meetings are the only oc-
casions when I've found it is possible for people to speak
about death as a fact of life. The mood of the meetings is
upbeat. My local chapter meetings are usually attended
by about forty members, many of them elderly, but with
a sprinkling of younger people eager, for whatever reason,
to exchange information about ways and means to die.
There is an inevitable cloak-and-dagger element to these
gatherings, given that mere advice regarding suicide has
the potential to be construed as a criminal offence. But
this only adds to the atmosphere of bravado and high
spirits. And of course there is humour. Did we all hear
about Tom, nudging ninety, who decided to take his helium bottle up to his local cemetery and gas himself there?
Apparently he figured the dead are unshockable. And, by
the way, anyone who is interested in a refresher course
on helium, please sign on for the upcoming workshop as
soon as possible as numbers are limited. It might be any
meeting of any common interest group, a bowls club, or a

bird-watching fraternity, except that, after the tea-break, it's back to rating cyanide and nitrogen gas according to ease of use, and speed.

The chief benefit of these meetings to me is their spirit of camaraderie. It takes courage to contemplate one's own death, and, as I said before, it is inexpressibly lonely. To find companions who share your desire to know more, to take the initiative, and to laugh in the face of our shared mortality, is a gift. How different from the experience of the hospital waiting room, where you sit in a glum herd with the overhead televisions blaring, guarding your dirty little secret until such time as your name is called. Whether it's good news or bad, the message is the same. In hospitals we don't talk about death, we talk about treatment. I would come out of consultations feeling as if my humanity had been diminished by the encounter, as if I'd been reduced to my disease alone, as if everything else that defines me had fallen away. By contrast, I came home from my Exit meetings emboldened, convinced that Camus was right: suicide is the only serious philosophical question.

Exit encourages its members to keep the conversation going by forming smaller coffee-and-chat groups with friends. Ours is chaired by Jean, a sprightly widow in her early eighties, who lives not far from me, in Kangaroo Point. There's a cafe near her flat where we can sit outside at a secluded corner table. We like to avoid being overheard. Counting myself, we are six regulars. I get a lift to meetings with Andrew, who has kidney cancer, and Colin, who has early stage Alzheimer's disease. Tony arrives on the bike he manages to ride despite his Parkinson's shakes. And Carol drives an hour and a half from the suburbs of the Sunshine Coast. There is nothing physically the matter with Carol, but after years of abuse, both emotional and physical, from her husband, she survives on a cocktail of anti-depressants and anti-anxiety medications. Her mental suffering makes her question the value of going on. The talk is remarkably intimate. Everyone knows why we're there. It's to comfort one another, to offer companionship. We're like the last survivors on a sinking ship, huddled together for warmth.

I don't mean to give the impression that my companions are all hell-bent on doing themselves in at the first opportunity. In my experience, our meeting to discuss suicide does not imply that we're all firmly committed to ending our own lives. It is more that we wish to contemplate what it would be like if that option was available to us within the same type of regulatory framework that exists in countries where assisted dying is legal. But this is not to say that anyone I've talked to about choosing to end one's own life takes the matter lightly. We talk about this in the car driving home from our coffee-and-chat meeting. Even if they had the means, Andrew and Colin doubt they could ever go through with it.

"It's too selfish," says Andrew, and I agree, thinking of the lonely hotel room and the traumatised housemaid. "It's like you're just saying 'fuck you' to all your family and friends."

Which is why my drug remains unused, because of some moral qualm I share with Andrew about the harm one can inadvertently do to others, by going rogue and acting alone.

o

It surprises me that I have any qualms at all, since I have never thought of myself as a person of particularly high moral standards, and I have no formal religious background on which to hang a moral framework. And yet one cannot face death without reflecting on questions of religious faith, or the lack of it, and on matters of morality, or its absence. For instance, I wonder whether doctors here are discouraged from talking about death with their patients by the strictly scientific and secular nature of the way our medicine is taught and practised. It could be that other, older medical traditions might understand and embrace grief and loss better than we do. And I wonder about the morality of the government subsidising expensive experimental cancer drugs, when other worthy areas of research go begging. As an example, the last melanoma drug I took, between 2014 and 2015, was priced at $8,500 a dose, to be administered every three weeks, for an indefinite period. I was the beneficiary of a free compassionate release of the drug, but it was very soon listed on the Pharmaceutical Benefits Scheme and attracted government subsidy, despite its limited efficacy. Lastly, I question the religious motive driving opposition to assisted dying for terminally ill patients such as myself. Could it be that we, whether or not we have religious beliefs, are being obstructed in our desire to die well by people who believe that God frowns on individual choice in the manner of dying? Or worse still, that God intends us to suffer? I don't know the answers to any of these questions, but I think they're worth debating.

So many people ask about your religious beliefs when you're dying. I remember my general practitioner asking if I was religious, after I told him I was running out of treatment options. He had just written me a referral to a palliative care unit, which happened to be based at a Catholic hospital.

"Are you a church-goer?" he said.

"No."

"That's good."

I asked him why and he told me that in his experience people with religious beliefs have a harder time dying than non-believers like me.

"I can't be certain why this is," he said, "but it probably has to do with attitudes to pain, and whether a person believes it serves a purpose."

I told him that I was up for any and all forms of pain relief. "Or better still, just shoot me."

"I'll make a note," he said.

I duly showed up for my appointment with the palliative care specialist at the Catholic hospital. I wasn't predisposed to like the hospital after what my family doctor had said. And it didn't help that my mother's nursing home, also a Catholic institution, happened to be part of the same complex. So some of the despair I'd always felt visiting my mother shadowed me as I made my way up to the consulting rooms on the fifth floor. As soon as the lift doors opened there was the same smell as the nursing home next door, stale urine masked with something artificially floral, the two scents fusing into a cloying fug. A corridor led me past the chapel, the entrance to which was festooned with sombre paintings and photographs of deceased nuns. Naturally enough, there were crosses everywhere, and images of Christ, intended to provide comfort to the faithful. But the iconography put me off balance, as if I was about to sit a test for which I'd done no preparation.

My meeting with the doctor was less reassuring than I'd hoped, even though he was softly spoken and sympathetic enough. Sitting in on the meeting was an older woman, a nurse, who, like the doctor, rarely smiled. If this had been a school I was assessing, to see if it was suitable for my children, I would have decided against it instantly, but I was going through a far more bizarre exercise, trying to form a judgment about the place where I might soon have to die, and finding it disappointing, even frightening. I thought of my drug. If it came down to a choice between dying in this place and dying by my own hand, I knew which I'd prefer. It was only common sense.

Thankfully I have since found a palliative care specialist I like, and he has referred me to a home-nursing service run by Buddhists. The nurses aren't Buddhists but the organisation was established by, and is supported by, monks and nuns who have trained in Tibetan Buddhism. I have had a couple of visits from one of the nuns, not formal counselling sessions, but conversations about how I'm dealing with my situation. The question of religion has, of course, come up in these chats, but mainly because I'm curious to hear from the nun how she came by her faith. I gather it was a gradual process of realising what was right for her, and of studying and meditating for years before she was allowed to commence her formal training. What I am most curious to know is how she views death. I have already told her that I don't believe in an afterlife, but she begs to differ.

She describes to me how the body closes down at the end, leaving nothing behind but an essential spirit. Sometime after the body breathes its last, the spirit is released into the ether.

"I've been there," she tells me. "I've seen it over and over again."

"What happens next?" I ask.

"The spirit searches for its next physical embodiment."

"Why does it do that?"

"Desire."

I know enough about Buddhism to understand that desire is seen as a curse, and when the nun starts to describe the endless cycle of reincarnation that is the fate of the average soul, I can see why one might want to be rid of it. That is not the part of her story that interests me, however. It is her proposition that our essence is perceptible. She has seen a lot of people die. If she says she has witnessed the body give up the ghost, then who am I, a complete novice in the field, to argue? And if she's right, I want to know whether it makes a difference how we die—fast or slow, violently or peacefully, by accident or by our own hand?

"What do you think of assisted dying?" I ask.

"I'm against it," she says. I had a feeling she might be. I have yet to come across anyone involved in palliative care who isn't against it. But I like the nun, so I am not about to argue with her. I like how serene she is, and how she looks directly at me when she speaks. I have even decided to invite her to say a prayer at my funeral, one she has picked out from *The Tibetan Book of Living and Dying*. It strikes me that this might provide an element of ritual to the occasion that might otherwise be missing.

For this is one of the most lamentable consequences of our reluctance to talk about death. We have lost our common rituals and our common language for dying, and must either improvise, or fall back on traditions about which we feel deeply ambivalent. I am talking especially about people like me, who have no religious faith. For us it seems that dying exposes the limitations of secularism like nothing else. I felt this most acutely when I turned to psychology for some advice. My family doctor had mentioned that I was eligible to receive free psychological help from the Cancer Council if I needed it.

"Six hour-long sessions, with more available if required."

"Why not?" I said.

He brought up a referral form on his computer.

"We just have to decide what to call your problem," he said.

"Dying," I said.

"Insufficient."

He silently scanned the list of problems for which help was available.

"Adjustment disorder."

I laughed. "You're making that up," I said.

He turned his computer screen so I could see for myself.

I sat with the psychologist in a windowless meeting room furnished with brightly coloured lounge chairs. A box of tissues was placed handily on a side table, along with a long glass of chilled water. The psychologist looked to be in her early thirties, pretty, neatly dressed. She took notes as I told her the history of my disease up to now. She asked a few questions about my home life, about my husband and children, about my daily routine. She asked if I was sleeping, eating, exercising, whether I had any fears.

"Of course," I said. "I'm frightened of dying."

"That's perfectly normal. How do you deal with your fears?"

"I try to think about other things. I read, I watch television, I see friends."

"Have you ever heard of mindfulness?"

I had heard of mindfulness. A counsellor visited me in hospital after my brain surgery. She took me through a few of the basic exercises: how to breathe, how to listen to the sounds around me, how to observe my thoughts as they passed.

"I use it sometimes," I said.

"It's good," she said, "to set aside time every day, to just enjoy the small things, the taste of an apple, the play of sunlight on the water, the smell of the rain."

"I know," I said, feeling a sudden urge to leave the room.

This was not what I'd come here to listen to. Surely this highly trained bright spark had something more up her professional sleeve than basic relaxation tips I could have picked up online any day of the week. I've read that the profession of psychologist is one of the forty or so predicted to disappear in the near future, along with bus driver and hotel receptionist. The research says that people are now more forthcoming about their problems when they're communicating virtually rather than face to face. Or perhaps it is because people like me expect more of psychologists than they can possibly deliver, some superior wisdom about the mysteries of life and death. It was a good thing I wasn't paying for my counselling, I thought, or I might have asked for my money back.

I ran out of things to say. Obviously I wasn't a particularly challenging patient, my adjustment disorder being mild to non-existent.

"Really I'm just sad," I said, trying to wrap up the session. "About all the things I've lost. I could have had another good ten years. But then, as Sartre says, everybody dies too early or too late."

The psychologist nodded. I'm not sure she had heard of Sartre, or rated his opinion on anything. "Grief can accumulate," she said. "Little losses one after the other can mount up. Perhaps that's something we can talk about next time." She closed her notebook to signal that my hour was up.

"You can book your next appointment at reception."

"Thanks," I said, although I had no intention of coming back.

The psychologist was right about one thing. Losses do mount up. Sometimes, when I'm sitting on the front verandah being mindful, I'll be distracted by the sight of a couple out on their evening walk. They'll be heading for the river, which isn't far from our house. There's a park down there that runs along the riverbank for a good three or four kilometres. I would walk with my husband along that stretch of the river every morning and evening. It was how we bookended the day. The water is never the same, sometimes calm, sometimes rough, sometimes rushing out to sea, at other times racing in. We might stop to watch a mother duck guide her ducklings to shore, or a cormorant on a fishing expedition. As the evening sky darkens, the fruit bats come streaming across in the hundreds from their rookeries on the far bank to the giant figs on this side. We don't do that walk anymore. I'm frightened I'll fall and break something. Nor do I ride my bike along there, another pleasure gone. With envy, I watch the passing cyclists, gliding along the way I used to, pedalling hard when they come to the hill. I even envy drivers. I had to give up driving after my brain surgery, because of the risk that I might have another seizure. How I'd love to pack the car and head off to some deserted beach for a swim. But I weigh less than my neighbour's retriever. I'd never make it beyond the first break. And so it goes, the endless list of pleasures I can no longer enjoy. Pointless to miss them of course, as that won't bring them back, but so much sweetness is bound to leave a terrible void when it's gone. I'm only grateful I tasted so much of it when I had the chance. I have had a blessed life in that way, full of countless delights. When you're dying, even your unhappiest memories can induce a sort of fondness, as if delight is not confined to the good times, but is woven through your days like a skein of gold thread.

o

You do reflect on your past when you're dying. You look for patterns and turning points and wonder if any of it is significant. You have the urge to relate the story of your life for your children so that you can set the record straight, and so that they can form some idea of where they came from. In recognition of this need, my home-nursing service employs volunteers called biographers, who visit patients, record their stories, then put together a bound copy of the finished product to present to the families of the dying.

Susan Addison was my biographer. She came every Wednesday for more than three months to listen to my tales of triumph and failure, during which time we became more like friends than volunteer and patient. It was a happy coincidence that we were both interested in books and writing. Susan had a daughter who was a screenwriter in Sydney and knew some of the same people I'd known when I'd lived there and worked in the same job. Having a lot in common, we talked quite freely during our sessions together, and I came to learn almost as much about Susan's history as she learned about mine. Very early on, for instance, she told me she had lost her only son to brain cancer when he was nineteen, a loss she had written about in her published memoir, *Mother Lode*.

She lent me a copy and I read it with a mounting sense of humility and respect. For someone like me, who knew so little about death, it was chastening to read this beautiful, unsentimental chronicle of someone who knew so much about it. Soon after her son's death, Susan had lost a number of other close family members in quick succession, and it had made her something of an expert in grief. But in spite of her losses she had refused to succumb to self-pity. She'd had help, she told me. After some searching around for spiritual solace, she had joined the Quakers and was a regular member at their meetings. It was the silence of the Quaker meetings she liked, she said, preferring it to services where there were sermons and singing. And she had the support of a loving husband, to whom she had been happily married for more than forty years.

Under the circumstances, Susan's attentiveness to my ramblings about my own life was flattering. None of my past troubles could compete with the death of a child, not my parents' messy divorce, or my own romantic flounderings, or my failures and setbacks as a writer. Mine was the privileged tale of someone who had not truly suffered. The fact that I was dying now was sad, but not tragic. I had lived a full life. Susan's son had died on the brink of manhood. The two deaths didn't bear comparison. This fact reminded me over and over again that my circumstances were less a cause for sorrow than an opportunity to feel thankful for my unearned good fortune. My two sons were still alive. I would not have to outlive them the way Susan had had to outlive her son. That alone was an immeasurable comfort to me. And I think Susan knew that. I think she understood that she wasn't just my chronicler, but my guide, my travel adviser to that bitter country she had already traversed a number of times before me.

And then one Wednesday Susan didn't turn up. I waited for her to call to say she was running late, but no call came. I heard nothing for a day, until Leanne from the nursing service rang me with the saddest possible news. Susan had suffered a massive stroke and was in hospital.

"It's not looking good," said Leanne. "I'm so sorry."

"I don't believe you," I said. "I was the one who was supposed to die."

"I know. We're all in shock. I'll let you know as soon as I hear anything."

A few days later Leanne rang me to say Susan had never recovered consciousness.

"That's ridiculous," I said. "She was sitting at my kitchen table a week ago laughing, telling stories."

"I'm sorry," said Leanne.

"I've got two books of hers," I said, as if the thought of her precious books might bring Susan back from the dead. The books were coffee-stained, scribbled in. She would want them returned.

"I'll let her daughter know," said Leanne. "Maybe she could pick them up."

"Please do."

Susan's daughter rang and cried down the phone. "Shit, shit, shit, shit."

I couldn't find any words to comfort her. I just told her how much her mother had helped me over the past few months.

"It was a privilege knowing her," I said.

"Thank you."

She picked up the books a couple of days before Christmas. So like her mother, tall, softly spoken, self-possessed.

"It used to be the four of us," she said. "Now it's down to Dad and me."

I asked her how her father was.

"Not great," she said. "It was all so sudden."

Everyone said the same thing. It was so sudden, so unpredictable, a reminder to all of us that life is fragile. True, but it wasn't how it was meant to be. Susan was supposed to bear witness to my passing, not the other way round. I was sorry we hadn't recorded her life story instead of

mine during our meetings. I was sorry she hadn't had the
same chance that I've had, to say a long goodbye to those
she loved, or to prepare them for life without her, to the
extent that that is possible. A sudden death cuts out all of
the ghastly preliminaries, but I imagine it leaves behind a
terrible regret for all the things left permanently unspo-
ken. A slow death, like mine, has that one advantage. You
have a lot of time to talk, to tell people how you feel, to try
to make sense of the whole thing, of the life that is coming to a close, both for yourself and for those who remain.

o

A few months back I was invited to take part in a program
for ABC television called *You Can't Ask That*. The premise
of the show is that there are taboo subjects about which
it is difficult to have an open and honest conversation,
death being one of them. The producer of the program
explained that I would be required to answer a number of
questions on camera. She said questions had been sent in
from all over the country, and the ten most common had
been selected. I wasn't to know what these were until the
day I went into the studio for the filming.

"They're written on cards and placed facedown on the
table," she said. "You're to pick up one card at a time, read
out the question, then answer it."

"I'll do my best," I said, more than willing to help. I've
never been a confident public speaker. I've always been

stymied by an uncomfortable suspicion that I was only posing as an expert. But in this case there could be no doubt. I knew about dying. In case my medical file wasn't proof enough, you only had to look at my ravaged face. And I agreed with the premise. Death is a taboo subject, absurdly so. It is tidied away in hospitals, out of public view, the secret purview of health professionals who are generally unwilling to talk about what really goes on at the bedsides of the nation.

It turned out that the producer of the program herself had a need to talk about death, as she had recently lost her father to cancer, and was struggling to cope. This is so often the case with people I talk to about my situation: they listen for a while, then they tell me their own death story, but always with a vague sense that it is shameful, that the whole sorry business is somehow their fault. In taking part in *You Can't Ask That*, I wanted to do my bit to change things around, to win back some dignity for the dying, because I don't think silence serves the interests of any of us.

The questions, as it turned out, were unsurprising. Did I have a bucket list, had I considered suicide, had I become religious, was I scared, was there anything good about dying, did I have any regrets, did I believe in an afterlife, had I changed my priorities in life, was I unhappy or depressed, was I likely to take more risks given that I was dying anyway, what would I miss the most, how would I like to be remembered? These were the same questions I'd been asking myself ever since I was diagnosed with cancer back in 2005. And my answers haven't changed since then. They are as follows.

No, I don't have a bucket list. From the age of fifteen, my one true ambition in life was to become a writer. I started out by writing schoolgirl poetry, heavily influenced by Robert Lowell, whom we were reading in class at the time. I had a massive crush on Geoff Page, my English teacher, who used to recite Lowell to us in class in his laconic drawl. It made my heart swell to hear him and I entered into a kind of delirium that compelled me to sit up late at night scribbling my own Lowellesque creations, convinced that, in the ordering of words, I had found my true vocation. Later I moved from poetry to screenwriting, then to writing for children, and finally to writing fiction. I published two novels and a handful of short stories. It wasn't a stellar career, although I did manage to collect a few outstanding mentors and friends along the way, as well as some loyal fans. So, in that sense, I count myself lucky. My real good fortune, however, was in discovering what I loved to do early in my life. It is my bliss, this thing called writing, and it has been since my schooldays. It isn't just the practice that enthralls me, it's everything else that goes with it, all the habits of mind.

Writing, even if most of the time you are only doing it in your head, shapes the world, and makes it bearable. As a schoolgirl, I thrilled at the power of poetry to exclude everything other than the poem itself, to let a few lines of verse make a whole world. Writing for film is no different. Emma Thompson once said that writing a screenplay was like trying to organise a mass of stray iron filings. You have to make the magnetic field so strong that it imposes its own order and holds the world of the screenplay in its tense, suspenseful grip. In fiction you can sometimes be looser and less tidy, but for much of the time you are choosing what to exclude from your fictional world in order to make it hold the line against chaos. And that is what I'm doing now, in this, my final book: I am making a shape for my death, so that I, and others, can see it clearly. And I am making dying bearable for myself.

I don't know where I would be if I couldn't do this strange work. It has saved my life many times over the years, and it continues to do so now. For while my body is careering towards catastrophe, my mind is elsewhere, concentrated on this other, vital task, which is to tell you something meaningful before I go. Because I'm never happier than when I'm writing, or thinking about writing, or watching the world as a writer, and it has been this way from the start.

If I had a secondary ambition growing up it was to travel. And I've done a lot of that, starting out with childhood expeditions led by my peripatetic father, then going it alone, then teaming up with a husband who is afflicted with the same wanderlust as I am. If anything, I've done too much moving around, to the point where I sometimes envy people who have stayed in the same place all their lives and put down deep roots. I blame my restlessness on Dad. He was an airline pilot who was happiest in mid-flight, neither here nor there. As soon as he hit the ground he felt trapped. His flightiness was the chief influence on my childhood. He moved constantly, from job to job, town to town, country to country. To me this seemed like a natural way to live. I revelled in the constant change, the excitement, the challenge of adapting to new situations. It made me resilient and agile. If there was a cost to it all, I wasn't too concerned, at least not until my parents' marriage fell apart under the strain.

As soon as I was able to, I started travelling on my own. I didn't have much of a purpose in mind, merely to see what was out there. I can still remember the green canvas bag I bought for my first solo trip. Compact and sturdy, it was a nod to my father's oft-repeated advice to travel light. I was headed for England, like so many others of my generation, drawn to a country we thought we knew from reading about it and seeing it on television. But travel, as well as being exhilarating, is also a process of disillusionment, of measuring your expectations against a very different reality. As I rode the train from Heathrow into London, I saw a landscape stripped of all enchantment, barely breathing under a dull sky, and felt my spirits dip. It was not exactly a disappointment, more a recognition that, in leaving home, I'd merely exchanged one enigma for another.

Of all my travels, the ones I've enjoyed the most have been to places I knew nothing about. Especially my first trip to Japan back in 1982. I had no preconceptions about the place apart from travel-poster visions of cherry blossoms and bullet trains. I arrived in the dead of night, disembarking at Narita Airport, which at the time was under siege from angry neighbourhood farmers opposed to its expansion. But I didn't know that, so I had no idea why the terminal was surrounded by razor wire and guarded by riot police decked out in samurai-style armour. I stared out of the bus window, transfixed, taking in the scene in all its fascinating detail, trying to fathom what might be going on. Guesswork, all guesswork, and it remained that way over the days and weeks to come, as I struggled with this most unfamiliar country, this empire of signs, as Roland Barthes so aptly dubbed it. Was I reading the signs right, or getting things hopelessly wrong? These were real-life questions when the problem was reaching the right destination along a train line, or emerging from an underground station at the right exit.

I've never lost my wonderment at Japan. I've travelled around the country many times since that first trip and I still thrill at the sights and sounds and smells: the sugary cloud of charcoal smoke billowing from the grilled eel shop, the soupy vapour you inhale with your ramen, the cut-straw sweetness of new tatami mats.

My point is that I've travelled enough, collected enough treasured memories to be satisfied. You can never go everywhere and see everything. Even if you did, I suspect there would be a point where you grew satiated with travel and longed to be home. Because the pleasures of home can be just as great as the pleasures of travel, and there is a price to be paid for wanting to be everywhere and nowhere, like my father. When he couldn't fly anymore Dad was lost. He had no other interests, nothing to ground him. I'm told that during his last confused days he fretted about his long-lost flight log books. At times he became so anxious about their whereabouts he had to be sedated.

A bucket list implies a lack, a store of unfulfilled desires or aspirations, a worry that you haven't done enough with your life. It suggests that more experience is better, whereas the opposite might equally be true. I don't have a bucket list because it comforts me to remember the things I have done, rather than hanker after the things I haven't done. Whatever they are, I figure they weren't for me, and that gives me a sense of contentment, a sort of ballast as I set out on my very last trip.

Yes, I have considered suicide, and it remains, for the reasons I have detailed, a constant temptation. If the law in Australia permitted assisted dying I would be putting plans into place right now to take my own life. Once the day came, I'd invite my family and closest friends to come over and we'd have a farewell drink. I'd thank them all for everything they've done for me. I'd tell them how much I love them. I imagine there would be copious tears. I'd hope there would be some laughter. There would be music playing in the background, something from the soundtrack of my youth. And then, when the time was right, I'd say goodbye and take my medicine, knowing that the party would go on without me, that everyone would stay a while, talk some more, be there for each other for as long as they wished. As someone who knows my end is coming, I can't think of a better way to go out. Nor can I fathom why this kind of humane and dignified death is outlawed.

No, it would not be breaking the law to go out on my own. The newspapers are full of options: hanging, falling from a great height, leaping in front of a speeding train, drowning, blowing myself up, setting myself on fire, but none of them really appeals to me. Again I'm constrained by the thought of collateral damage, of the shock to my family, of the trauma to whoever was charged with putting out the flames, fishing out the body, scraping the brains off the pavement. When you analyse all the possible scenarios for suicide, none of them is pretty. Which is the reason I support the arguments in favour of assisted

dying, because, to misquote Churchill, it is the worst
method of dying, except for all the others.

No, I haven't become religious; that is, I haven't experienced a late conversion to a particular faith. If that means
I'm going straight to hell when I die then so be it. One
of my problems with religion has always been the idea
that the righteous are saved and the rest are condemned.
Isn't that the ultimate logic of religion's "us" and "them"
paradigm?

Perhaps it's a case of not missing what you have never
had. I had no religious instruction growing up. I knew
a few Bible stories from a brief period of attendance at
Sunday school, but these seemed on a level with fairy
tales, if less interesting. Their sanctimoniousness put me
off. I preferred the darker tones of the Brothers Grimm,
who presented a world where there was no redemption,
where bad things happened for no reason, and nobody
was punished. Even now I prefer that view of reality. I
don't think God has a plan for us. I think we're a species
with godlike pretensions but an animal nature, and that,
of all of the animals that have ever walked the earth, we
are by far the most dangerous.

Cancer strikes at random. If you don't die of cancer
you die of something else, because death is a law of nature. The survival of the species relies on constant renew-
al, each generation making way for the next, not with any

improvement in mind, but in the interests of plain endurance. If that is what eternal life means then I'm a believer. What I've never believed is that God is watching over us, or has a personal interest in the state of our individual souls. In fact, if God exists at all, I think he/she/it must be a deity devoted to monumental indifference, or else, as Stephen Fry says, why dream up bone cancer in children?

Yes, I'm scared, but not all the time. When I was first diagnosed I was terrified. I had no idea that the body could turn against itself and incubate its own enemy. I had never been seriously ill in my life before; now suddenly I was face to face with my own mortality. There was a moment when I saw my body in the mirror as if for the first time. Overnight my own flesh had become alien to me, the saboteur of all my hopes and dreams. It was incomprehensible, and so frightening, I cried.

"I can't die," I sobbed. "Not me. Not now."

But I'm used to dying now. It's become ordinary and unremarkable, something everybody, without exception, does at one time or another. If I'm afraid of anything it's of dying badly, of getting caught up in some process that prolongs my life unnecessarily. I've put all the safeguards in place. I've completed an advanced health directive and given a copy to my palliative care specialist. I've made it clear in my conversations, both with him and with my family, that I want no life-saving interventions at the end, nothing designed to delay the inevitable. My doctor has promised to honour my wishes, but I can't help worrying. I haven't died before, so I sometimes get a bad case of beginner's nerves, but they soon pass.

No, there is nothing good about dying. It is sad beyond belief. But it is part of life, and there is no escaping it. Once you grasp that fact, good things can result. I went through most of my life believing death was something that happened to other people. In my deluded state I imagined I had unlimited time to play with, so I took a fairly leisurely approach to life and didn't really push myself. At least that is one explanation for why it took me so long to write my first novel. There were others. I had been trying to write the story of my parents for years, making character notes, outlining plots, embarking on one false start after another. But again and again I failed to breathe life into the thing, constrained by the fact that my parents were still alive to read what I had written.

Once my parents were dead I didn't have to worry so much. I could say what I liked about them without hurting their feelings. And once I knew that my own death was looming, I could no longer make any excuses. It was now or never. I wouldn't say that made the writing of my novel *Me and Mr. Booker* any easier, but it spurred me on. This was my only chance to leave for posterity a piece of work that was truly mine. For years I'd worked on screenplays, but that was a collaborative process. And it is usual for screenplays to disappear into a bottom drawer, never to be seen again. I know that novels disappear too, but at least they still exist, whole works, whether hard copy or digital, as objects, and that has always been their appeal for me. A book stands alone. A screenplay is only a suggestion for a story, but a novel is the thing itself.

It was a feeling like no other, in late 2011, to hold a copy of my first novel in my hand. When Patricia Highsmith's publisher sent her copies of her first novel, *Strangers on a Train*, she couldn't believe how much space they occupied. It seemed so brazen to have made an object that took up room in the world. I knew what Highsmith meant. I'd stuck my neck out at last, staked my claim to be taken seriously as a writer, and here in my hand was the proof. Now, I thought, I can die happy.

Yes, I have regrets, but as soon as you start rewriting your past you realise how your failures and mistakes are what define you. Take them away and you're nothing. But I do wonder where I'd be now if I'd made different choices, if I'd been bolder, smarter, more sure of what I wanted and how to get it. As it was, I seemed to stumble around, making life up as I went along. Looking back, I can make some sense of it, but at the time my life was all very makeshift and provisional, more dependent on luck than on planning or intent.

Still, as the British psychotherapist and essayist Adam Phillips says, we are all haunted by the life not lived, by the belief that we've missed out on something different and better. My favourite reverie is about the life I could have led in Paris if I'd chosen to stay there instead of returning home like I did. I was twenty-two. I'd run away. I was meant to be in Oxford studying for a postgraduate degree in history, but a few weeks into the first term I decided to quit. I found Oxford both intimidating and dull. My supervisor was an expert in the constitutional history of New South Wales, and he was keen for me to assist with his research. He could see I was struggling and he meant to be kind, but his offer felt more like a punishment than a helping hand, and I prevaricated.

I had a standing invitation from my cousin and his wife to visit them in Paris, so I emptied my bank account and bought a ticket. I remember standing on the deck of the ferry leaving Folkestone one blustery November afternoon and thinking that my life had just begun, that this was the start of my great adventure. France had always had a magical allure for me, ever since my high-school French classes with the effete Mr. Collins. He made us draw maps of the country showing all the main rivers, geographical features, and agricultural products. It seemed a land of such plenitude; I vowed to go there one day and see it for myself. As a sort of preparation for the voyage out Mr. Collins gave each of us a French name. Mine was

Jeanne. I took my new name as an invitation to adopt a whole new persona in a new language, someone more sophisticated and worldly than I was, a girl who knew her way around. It was the possibility of reinvention that I was drawn to—just as I still am. As soon as I stepped onto French soil I sensed my high-school alter ego spring back into life. Jeanne bought a packet of Gauloises to celebrate and smoked them on the train, while reading her copy of Marguerite Duras's *The Lover*. If only I could write like that, she thought, instantly dismissing her lingering doubts about quitting the academic life.

My cousin met me on Rue Mouffetard and I followed him around while he bought the ingredients for dinner. So many cheeses, wines, pastries, charcuterie. So much seafood, all so fresh it gleamed. And so much beauty, in the passing faces, in the sensual language, in the storybook houses winding down the hill. I could barely breathe for happiness. I could have stayed if I'd really wanted to. I was broke, but I could have found work if I'd tried. My cousin taught English, or I suppose there were au pair agencies I might have telephoned. I spoke bad French, but I could have learned the language. In fact, after two or three enchanted days, I went back to Oxford and investigated switching to an undergraduate course in French and Spanish, only to discover it wasn't possible on my meagre resources. I could have asked my mother for a loan, but she was already in debt because of her divorce.

And so I gave up on Paris and came home, imagining another chance might come one day to make my move, to slip into Jeanne's skin and write my astonishing novels in my 5th arrondissement garret. No such luck. Naturally. But then that turned out to be fortunate, because other opportunities arose soon enough, as they do, and other chances to reinvent myself in ways I could never have predicted.

The problem with reverie is that you always assume you know how the unlived life turns out. And it is always a better version of the life you've actually lived. The other life is more significant and more purposeful. It is impossibly free of setbacks and mishaps. This split between the dream and the reality can be the cause of intense dissatisfaction at times. But I am no longer plagued by restlessness. Now I see the life I've lived as the only life, a singularity, saturated with its own oneness. To envy the life of the alternative me, the one who stayed in Paris, or the one who became an expert in the constitutional history of New South Wales, seems like the purest kind of folly.

No, I don't believe in an afterlife. Dust to dust, ashes to ashes sums it up for me. We come from nothingness and return to nothingness when we die. That is one meaning of the circle beloved of calligraphers in Japan, just a big bold stroke, starting at the beginning and travelling back to it in a round sweep. In my beginning is my end says T. S. Eliot.

Old fires to ashes, and ashes to the earth / Which is already flesh, fur and faeces / Bone of man and beast, cornstalk and leaf. When I first read *Four Quartets* at school it was like a revelation. The world was just as he described it and no other way, a place where beauty and corruption cohabit and are often indistinguishable.

When the Buddhist nun who sometimes visits me asked me if I believed in an afterlife I said I thought we are only remembered for so long, by the people who knew us, and that after friends and family are gone we're forgotten. I told her about the cemeteries in the Japanese porcelain town Arita, where my husband and I have bought a house. The town officially dates back four hundred years, but presumably there were farmers there before the potters arrived. Way past its heyday, Arita is now host to far more dead than living inhabitants, so that whatever route you take through its narrow, winding streets you soon come upon graveyards packed with monuments to the deceased. It's easy to tell which of them are remembered, because some graves are beautifully kept and often visited. It's just as easy to tell which of the dead have been completely forgotten, as their graves are crumbling and overgrown with weeds. In some corners you'll even find memorial stones jumbled together willy-nilly, unceremoniously sidelined to make space for newcomers.

I told the nun that Shin, a painter, had decided to move to Arita because he liked the idea of painting on porcelain instead of on perishable materials like paper or canvas. Arita is littered with porcelain shards everywhere you look. All around the old kiln sites you pick up bits of blue and white porcelain plates, cups, teapots. The bed of the river that runs through the town is layered with discarded bits of porcelain, pieces of pots that cracked in the firing or were found wanting in some other way and were simply flung out the windows of the workshops into the water. Shin likes to imagine that four hundred years from now shards of his work might be unearthed and collected by some curious traveller, just as he likes to unearth and collect fragments of work painted by his predecessors. In that way, he says, he will have achieved a degree of immortality. I say that I feel the same way about my work. I like to think that, long after I'm gone, someone somewhere might read a book or essay of mine in a last remaining library or digital archive and be touched in some way.

The nun listens politely to my theories of the afterlife but I can tell she doesn't agree with me. I get the feeling that for her things are not as simple as I describe them. I don't pretend to understand her belief system but I imagine it assumes the existence of another place, separate from this one. What else can she mean when she describes the essential spirit departing the body for the "ether"? This is where religion gets too cryptic for me, or maybe it's just that language is inadequate to describe the indescribable.

I'm much more drawn to all of the ordinary ways in which we cheat death. It might be through the evocative power of the objects we leave behind, or it might be in a form of words, a turn of the head, a way of laughing. I was sitting at dinner the other night with some very old friends of ours. They'd met my mother many times, back when she was still herself, before she became ill. The wife looked hard at me for a while.

"You get more and more like her," she said.

It felt for a moment as if my mother had joined us, that us all being together had conjured up her presence at the table. It was only a fleeting thing. But then I can't imagine an afterlife that consists of anything more than these brief and occasional visits with the living, these memories that come unbidden and out of nowhere, then vanish again into oblivion.

No, my priorities remain the same. Work and family. Nothing else has ever really mattered to me. It might sound odd for a writer with my small output to claim that work has been a lifelong preoccupation, but it's true. When I wasn't actually writing I was preparing to write, rehearsing ideas, reading, observing life and character, learning from other writers. As Nora Ephron always said, everything is copy. If I was slower than some at finding success, it isn't because I wasn't trying. I was trying and failing all the time. That's what I'm doing now and I hope failing better. I've put off using my death as material for a long time, mainly because I couldn't find the right tone. I'm not even sure I've found it now.

To say that family has been my other chief priority in life is to understate the case. Marriage, children, the whole catastrophe as Zorba called it. To become a mother is to die to oneself in some essential way. After I had children I was no longer an individual separate from other individuals. I leaked into everyone else. I remember going to a movie soon after Nat was born and walking out at the first hint of violence. It was unbearable to think of the damage done. I had never been squeamish in my life before, but now a great deal more was at stake. I had delivered a baby into the world. From now on my only job was to protect and nurture him into adulthood, no matter what it cost me. This wasn't a choice. It was a law.

That makes it sound like a selfless task, but it wasn't. I got as much as I gave, and much more. The ordinary pleasures of raising children are not often talked about, because they are unspectacular and leave no lasting trace, but they sustained me for years as our boys grew and flourished, and they continue to sustain me now. I can't help but take pleasure in the fact that my children are thriving as I decline. It seems only fitting, a sure sign that my job in the world is done. It's like the day Dan, then in the fourth grade, turned to me twenty yards from the school gate and said, "You can go now,

Mum." I knew then that the days of our companionable walks were over, and that as time went by there would be further signs of my superfluity, just as poignant and necessary as this one.

No, I am not unhappy or depressed, but I am occasionally angry.

Why me? Why now? Dumb questions but that doesn't stop me from asking them. I was supposed to defy the statistics and beat this disease through sheer willpower. I was supposed to have an extra decade in which to write my best work. I was robbed!

Crazy stuff. As if any of us are in control of anything. Far better for me to accept that I am powerless over my fate, and that for once in my life I am free of the tyranny of choice. That way I waste a lot less time feeling singled out or cheated.

As I told the young psychologist, I rely on friends to divert me from dark thoughts. I don't have a lot of friends, but the ones I do have are so good to me, so tender and solicitous, it would seem ungrateful to subside into unhappiness or depression. And then there's Shin, without whom I'd be lost. He's been so good-humoured and loving; I owe him no less than my sanity. If I'm ever depressed or unhappy, I hide the fact from him as best I can. It's the least I can do.

No, I'm not likely to take more risks in life, now that I know I'm dying. I'm not about to tackle skydiving or paragliding. I've always been physically cautious, preternaturally aware of all the things that can go wrong when one is undertaking a dangerous activity. Paradoxically, it was Dad who taught me to be careful. I don't think he was temperamentally suited to flying; the risks played unhealthily on his mind and made him fearful, tetchy, depressed. At the same time he was addicted to the thrill of flying and couldn't give it up.

His ambivalence about danger confused me while I was growing up. He never discouraged me from taking up risky activities; instead he filled me with fear about the possible consequences, with the result that I was never any good at them. When he taught me to drive, he made sure to emphasise the fallibility of the machine, something he would have learned during the war at flying school, where mistakes could be fatal. He liked to open the bonnet of the car before we set off, and run through a sort of flight check with me to make sure everything was hooked up to everything else. These were good lessons and they've served me well, but I wonder if a certain enthusiasm for risk drained out of me as a result of his teaching methods, and whether that wasn't his intent. It strikes me that I might have turned out differently if he'd taken me for a spin one day in one of the Tiger Moths he loved so much, shown me what had turned him on to flying in the first place, emphasised the mad joy rather than the danger.

The irony is that, despite my never having tempted death the way daredevils do, I'm dying anyway. Perhaps it is a mistake to be so cautious. I sometimes think this is the true reason for my reluctance to take my own life. It is because suicide is so dangerous.

I shall miss you so much when I'm dead: Harold Pinter, dying of cancer, speaking of his wife. I know exactly what he means.

The short answer to the question of what I'll miss the most is Shin, my husband of thirty-one years, and the faces of my children.

The long answer is the world and everything in it: wind, sun, rain, snow, and all the rest.

And I will miss being around to see what happens next, how things turn out, whether my children's lives will prove as lucky as my own.

But I will not miss dying. It is by far the hardest thing I have ever done, and I will be glad when it's over.

I'd like to be remembered by what I've written. As somebody once warned, if you don't tell your own story, someone else will.

But I know I have no real say in how I will be remembered. It is in the nature of memory that different people will remember different things, and that none of what they remember will be verifiable or true. This is the case even in my own recollections about my life, which are porous and mutable and open to contradictory interpretations. If I use them in my work, which I often do, it is to fit them into a particular narrative, to shape them to a purpose, because that is how fiction is made. In the process, I become convinced that the fictional version of my memory is the real version, or at least preferable to it. It is a thoroughly self-serving exercise, I know, but that is part of its attraction.

In the end it is a blessing to be remembered at all, and we should not worry too much about how or why. My grandmother on my mother's side died before I got to know her. But I remember her as a talented woman with literary aspirations who died too young to fulfil her potential—because that's what I heard so often from my mother. The point of the story was not lost on me. It was a cautionary tale, and it haunted me, as it haunted Mum. But to my mind it was also a romantic story, especially in the detail. My grandmother was a country girl from Longreach, in outback Queensland. When she was scarcely out of school, she married a grazier twelve years her senior. She wrote bush poetry that was published in the *Bulletin*, but her real wish was to escape to the city, to meet with other writers and be part of a literary scene. Her chance didn't come until she was sixty. Newly widowed, she bought herself an apartment at the Macleay Regis in Kings Cross, in the heart of bohemian Sydney.

A week or so after moving in she died in her sleep. A sad end, of course, but what impressed me was the strength of her ambition—she had nursed it for so long and against such odds. And I admired the fact that she took writing seriously, which gave me permission to do the same, to protect my own little flame of ambition as soon as it flared up in high school.

Without my grandmother's example, who knows what might have become of me? I might have dismissed poetry as a waste of time and concentrated on my science classes. As it was, a part of me always believed that I was honouring my grandmother's memory by choosing writing as a profession, that I was finishing something she had started, or at least taking up the baton. I know she is not aware of it, but I'm still persuaded she would be pleased to think that this is how she is remembered. In that way, too, she is a pioneer, gone ahead of me into the great bohemia in the ether.

II

DUST AND ASHES

I am the youngest of three children. My sister, Sarah, is six years older than I am, and my brother, Eliot, four years older. I have the impression that I was a surprise, if not a mistake. According to my mother, when she announced that she was pregnant for the third time, my grandmother shook her head in disbelief. "You stupid girl," she said, rightly worried about the state of my parents' marriage. For some reason, this story always made my mother laugh. I couldn't see the joke; maybe you had to have been there.

From time to time as we were growing up my mother would take Sarah and Eliot and me out to the place where she was born. We went in the winter school holidays, from Sydney, and later from Canberra. It was two or three days by car, up through New South Wales, and across the border into Queensland, the towns growing sparser and dustier the further we drove, the horizon flattening, the sky overhead broadening until there was so much of it your eyes ached from staring.

The pattern of our visits was always the same. We stayed with my mother's youngest sister, Jenny, and her husband, Ranald. They lived on North Delta, a sheep and cattle property near Barcaldine that had belonged to my grandfather Norman Murray. The country there was ochre, scrubby, and we approached it along a rutted road that my mother navigated gingerly because of the bull dust. I could tell she was scared as soon as she turned off the bitumen. She gripped the wheel and narrowed her gaze to a few feet ahead, expecting us to strike disaster at any moment. The bush wasn't her natural element. She might have been born there, but after years of exile she had become suburban and cautious.

At the end of such a long journey the homestead was always a joyous sight, set in a clearing surrounded by rough-hewn fences. We drove in from the back, passing the machinery shed and the chicken coops and the pigsty and the tethered dogs along the way. The verandahs were pitched wide and low, so from a distance the house appeared to be all red roof. Once you had come in through the kitchen door, you immediately saw the point of this arrangement. It meant the sun was barred entry, and inside was kept dark and shadowy as a cave.

There was no real logic to the design of Delta. Beyond the kitchen was a breakfast room, really just a screened section of the verandah, and beyond that a warren of rooms that had been added or partitioned over time to accommodate Jenny and Ranald and their four sons. Jenny would lead us through the rooms, allocating beds as she went, then serve us tea at the front of the house, where the verandah was at its widest and overlooked a lawn and a swimming pool.

It was here that the talk took place and all the stories were told. It was here that I learned where my mother had come from and why she carried such a burden of sadness. Not that this was much in evidence, for generally she was a person who liked to laugh and enjoy life, but underneath her vibrancy there was another strain, a sort of indelible grief that no amount of good cheer could dislodge. And this grief, it soon became clear, had originated in her Queensland childhood, to which she felt compelled to return periodically, with us in tow as her excuse.

It is notable that our father rarely came with us on these trips. Often, in the early days, he was away flying somewhere, but later he didn't come because my mother preferred to travel without him. There was a lot of talk on the verandah about Mum's hasty marriage to the handsome pilot she had met in a bar, and about how, in the intervening years, things had gone so disastrously wrong. I listened to these tales with extra attention. My father had told me so little about himself, and it was rare to hear from people like Jenny and Ranald who had known him since the start, so I took note, my writer's instincts already awakened, piecing together, guessing, inventing, trying to figure out what it all meant. My brother and sister preferred to be out on the horses with my cousins, but I was a reluctant rider and happier to sit astride a squatter's chair scoffing teacakes and soaking up the family legends.

I liked Jenny and Ranald. They were kind and funny. Every morning the giant AGA stove in the kitchen was fired up and spitting by daybreak. Ranald was the breakfast cook, frying up huge quantities of lambs fry, bacon, onions, eggs, first for the working men, who had to be away early, and then for us layabouts, who came to the table still sleepy at eight.

"Geez, did you ever see such a useless bunch?" he'd say. "Have to get you out cutting fence posts for a day or two. Then you'll know you're born."

We did go out with him some days, setting off in the truck to check a dam or repair a pump somewhere. Jenny would load us up with smoko: lumps of fruit cake, tins full of scones, tea for the billy. On the way, Ranald would talk about the weather or the price of beef, and his fears about the state of the nation. He was a fierce conservative, afraid of the communists, the unions, the Catholics, and he was convinced that the Chinese were intent on sweeping down from the north when nobody was looking. But he was not averse to a debate, and when my mother challenged his views he happily sparred with her as if it was a sport. He was also a lover of poetry and would recite Burns and Tennyson as he worked away sawing timber, or mending gates, his mellifluous voice echoing in the emptiness all around him. It made my mother cry to listen, which was why he did it, I was certain.

"You should never have gone away," he told her. "You should have married a good solid bloke from round here and been a plain country wife."

"And gone mad, just like Ril did," said my mother.

Ril was my grandmother. Back on the verandah, Jenny and Mum talked as much about her as they did about my father, often likening one to the other, as if they were part of the same problem, the suggestion being that my mother had married a man who reminded her of her own mother, and had paid the price. The image I formed of my grandmother, as I listened to them talk, was of a beautiful, haughty, irascible woman, incompetent as a mother, unhappy as a wife, beset by an unrelenting restlessness that saw her crack once or twice under the pressure of it all. Most notoriously, I learned, she had suffered a breakdown during the war and had spent some months in a clinic in Brisbane trying to get better. The cause was pretty clear: a son in the navy somewhere in the Pacific, my mother nursing in Townsville at an army hospital, my mother's other sister Judy already married at seventeen, and Jenny away at boarding school, no men to help out on the property, her husband out working alone from dawn till dusk, with all the attendant risks. He had come home one evening to find her packing her suitcases at random, stuffing

everything she owned into them, the rooms turned up-
side down.

My father's nervous breakdown had been less dra-
matic. I was just old enough to remember him taking to
his bed and refusing to get up for days and days. Perhaps
I took him up a sandwich occasionally, leaving it on the
bedside table for him to eat when he woke up. I seem to
remember him always asleep, his hair unwashed, his jowls
covered in dark stubble, his sheets stale. Jenny, who was
visiting us in Sydney at the time, recalled him sending
messages to my mother via a piece of string lowered from
his bedroom window to the kitchen below.

"He'd tie a note on the end," she told me, "requesting
a cup of tea and a biscuit."

My mother laughed bitterly.

"I made him an appointment to see a psychiatrist," she
said, "but he refused to go."

I was fascinated by these problem relatives, my grandmother with her restlessness, and my father with his in-
ability to stay in one place, until his nerves frayed so much
he couldn't move. I couldn't help wondering how much of
them might be in me, and whether cracking under pressure might be a family trait. I also wondered at the source
of their fragility, whether it was an inborn hypersensitiv-
ity to things, or bred of a justifiable rage at the conditions
under which they were forced to live. One of my mother's

theories was that they were both people with enormous untapped potential who had missed out on a proper education and therefore felt they could never catch up.

"Interesting that neither of them finished school," she said, explaining that my grandmother had been expelled from her Toowoomba boarding school in her final year, and that my father had been thrown out of home and school at the age of fifteen.

"The war saved him," she said. "He lied his way into the air force and never looked back."

As for my grandmother, she married at eighteen and had four children in the space of ten years. "Out here," said Mum, gesturing at the empty landscape beyond the fence, "with no one to talk to. No wonder she went nuts."

At some point during our visit, my mother's brother, Peter, and his wife, Jan, would telephone with an invitation to visit Beaconsfield for the day. In some ways this was the highlight of the trip, because Beaconsfield was the family home, the place where my mother and her brother and sisters had grown up. And yet we never stayed there. We only ever went for lunch.

"What's the bet she feeds us in the kitchen," said Mum, as we set out on one of these excursions. "Off paper plates."

I gathered there was no love lost between my mother and her sister-in-law. In a plot worthy of Jane Austen, Peter, as the only son, had inherited Beaconsfield outright, thus dispossessing his sisters of any claim to the place, other than a sentimental one. In this, according to Mum, he was enthusiastically aided and abetted by Jan, who had taken the extra step of suggesting that my grandmother was no longer welcome in her own home.

"That's why Ril took that round the world cruise," said my mother. "She had nowhere else to go. And then she came to stay with us in Ceduna."

I had only the vaguest recollection of Ceduna, on the South Australian coast. We had moved there briefly when I was four, when Dad landed a job with the Royal Flying Doctor Service. But I did remember the miniature tea set my grandmother had brought me from Hong Kong, and the dress with the gathering at the bodice that scratched in the desert heat. And I had seen the photograph of her descending regally from a DC3, her hair tied in a scarf, her eyes hidden behind enormous sunglasses, her sadness wafting around her like a private cloud.

"Poor Mum," said my mother. "She spent her days sitting on the sand staring out to sea. I don't think I'd ever seen anyone so lost."

Exile, I decided. That must be the explanation for my mother's grief. First her own exile from home, going way back to childhood, when she was sent to school in faraway Brisbane at the age of eight, but then later the spectacle of her mother's banishment from the place where

she had lived all of her adult life. And if I cared to go even
further back, which other women would I find, displaced,
banished, abandoned? Ril's mother for instance, whom I
knew only from stories, holed up in a rambling house in
Longreach where she waited hand and foot on Ril's bach-
elor brother Frank, in an effort, I imagine, to keep him
close. Grandma Cory was the one who was old enough,
when my mother knew her as a child, to recall spear attacks on the local squatters and the deadly retributions
that followed. Perhaps that was the original grief of anyone who came from out there, from those towns; it was
the grief for the exterminated, the poisoned, the diseased
and dispossessed. Perhaps no amount of forgetting could
fully expunge the memory of the original conquest, the
primal crime, gone forever unpunished, because there was
nobody left to bear witness or tell the tale.

I thought about that as we drove over to Beaconsfield
on one of our lunch dates. I must have been in high school
by then, and growing aware of my country's hidden history. It struck me that only two Aborigines had ever
featured in my mother's stories of her childhood. One
a young, nameless domestic servant who had been sent
from a mission to work for Ril shortly after her marriage
to Norman. The girl had taken fright and run away. The
other an old man known only as Bill, who had worked
for Norman for many years as a stockman and general
roustabout. My mother had a picture of Bill posing for

the photo beside a pony, with her sitting up on the saddle behind, aged three or four.

"He was devoted to Dad," she said. "Every morning he'd sit outside the study door until Dad came out and gave him his jobs. And then one day he was gone. Vanished."

The way she told these stories, Bill and the housemaid were more like apparitions than real people, ghosts returning briefly from some other world to lay claim on their country, only to disappear all over again, too distressed to stay.

The landscape changes somewhere between Barcaldine and Longreach. The trees disappear, the soil changes from ochre to bleached bone. Seen in a drought it can look like a moonscape, just a barren plain, but after rain it can turn into an ocean of grass. I gathered that Beaconsfield was better country than Delta, though I couldn't tell, knowing nothing of the exigencies of grazing. All I saw, turning onto the Beaconsfield road, was more featureless nothingness. Not so for my mother, who knew every inch of the road from years of travelling up and down it as a child. She remembered where it took a turn towards the dry creek bed, where it rose again to give you your first glimpse of the homestead, where it passed by the tombstone of the cowboy who had been struck dead on the spot by lightning over half a century ago. She was excited to be travelling the road again. I could tell by the way she sat forward in her seat and pointed out what was up ahead.

"That's where Dad bogged the car bringing me back from the train after I'd finished school. On the way home I said I wanted to go on to university. Waste of time. Full of communists, he said. We had to leave the car and walk the rest of the way, arguing."

There it was again. My mother's exile. She went to university in the end, somehow persuading her father to give her permission, and that marked her out, for the rest of her life, as dangerously over-educated, full of ideas that were foreign to her family. It made them afraid of her.

She gave a little cheer as the homestead appeared up ahead. It was conspicuously grander than Delta, although of the same basic design. A huge canopy of green tin over a sprawling structure that seemed without back or front, having expanded over the years out from the centre. A lush garden shaded the house on all sides, oasis-like in the middle of the scorched plain all around. Peter and Jan appeared on the garden path and waved in a gesture of welcome. They didn't look at all mean in the way I'd heard them described, just proprietorial, which was enough to rankle Mum.

"I'm surprised they don't charge us an entry fee," she said.

Peter put his arm around his wife's shoulder in a protective gesture and they advanced together through the gate to be there when the car pulled up.

"Welcome to Beaconsfield," he said, as if to a group of strangers, after which there was embracing and handholding, none of it especially warm. It was a contrast to Ranald, who almost lifted you off the ground when he met you, held you to his barrel chest so you could take in the working man smell of him.

"Come in, come in," said Jan. "Let us show you around."

The tour was for my mother's sake, to show off all of the changes that had taken place since her last visit. Rooms had been added, or joined together, or opened up, made more formal or more casual, redecorated according to Jan's taste. As I followed the group around I could see my mother growing more and more irritated, as if the whole exercise was a slap in the face. Peter had a way of referring to "my mother" and "my father", a slip she found so exasperating she corrected him more than once.

"Our mother," she said. "Our father."

But he took no notice. He was too busy showing off the formal dining room, which was furnished, according to my mother, with pieces she remembered from her childhood: the same long burnished table with the same solid chairs, the same sideboard heaving with silverware and china she recalled using as a girl. Peter wanted to let her know where the state governor had sat on his last visit, and which federal ministers had sat beside him, but my mother couldn't have cared less.

"This is where Ril used to sit," she told me, "whisky in hand. She had a way of rubbing her little finger against her ring finger, I remember. It was a sign she was about to blow up."

She sat in the chair and showed me the gesture, holding her head in the way her mother had. I had seen enough photographs of Ril to recognise the lift of the chin, the imperious stare.

"She faced your father down the length of this table once," she told me, "and demanded to know when he was going to give up adventuring and get a proper job."

"What did he say?"

"I shall avoid it as long as humanly possible."

"That's why they got on so well," said Jenny. "She didn't frighten him."

According to legend, my father had thoroughly charmed my grandmother, the same way he charmed everyone else. He played the dashing aviator, flying in once in a while for a surprise visit in a friend's plane, alighting on the Beaconsfield airstrip wearing jodhpurs and suede boots, tweaking the ends of his air force moustache, and dazzling all and sundry with his villainous smile.

"Errol Flynn, we called him," said Jenny.

"The boots were too much for Dad," said my mother. "He thought suede was code for queer. He even took me aside one night to caution me."

"Shall we have lunch now?" said Jan, discomforted by the turn of the conversation. I sensed that she found my mother unsettling, and not entirely respectable, that

Mum's visits were an ordeal to be endured rather than an occasion for celebration.

As Mum had predicted, we ate lunch in the kitchen, crammed into a corner breakfast nook where Jan had set out a salad and a plate of sandwiches on a small Formica table. The talk was mainly about rain and the lack of it, and about the fortunes of friends and neighbours who were doing it tough. My mother recognised some of the names and joined in, catching up on news of clans she had known of since girlhood, friends who had stayed behind when she left, and made their lives in the bush, while she was busy inventing an entirely different life elsewhere. Soon she grew restless at the table and excused herself.

"I just want to take a wander on my own," she said.

Later I found her lying flat on her back on the bare floorboards of the hallway that bisected the house straight down the middle, or had done before all of the additions and modifications had changed things around. At first I thought she had collapsed there.

"Are you okay?"

"I couldn't take any more of that incestuous gossip," she said. "Have you noticed how they never ask any questions about us? It's like nothing exists beyond the boundary fence."

I sat down beside her on the cool boards.

"Ril used to lie here on summer afternoons," she said, "to catch whatever breeze there was. She wouldn't speak, only to tell the nanny to keep us away."

I was reminded of my father's sulks, sometimes lasting two or three days, when he wouldn't say a word to anyone. I knew the fear this kind of silence can induce. You are convinced that it is your fault, that your very existence is a provocation. At least that was the case with Dad. He never hid the fact that he resented family life and found the demands of fatherhood intolerable. I gathered Ril had been the same, saddled with four children before she was fully grown herself, appalled at the sacrifice of her youth, and of any kind of autonomy, financial or emotional. No wonder my mother harboured so much grief. She must have imbibed it from birth, sucked it in with the very air. And here she was, back at the source, filling herself up with it again, as she lay sprawled on the floor in the spot where her mother had sulked and gone silent on all those blistering afternoons.

"Time to go," she said, hauling herself up to her feet. "I've seen enough."

Peter and Jan could barely disguise their relief as we readied to leave. They herded us to the gate and beamed as we piled into the car.

"Give my love to Ranald," they said, feigning politeness. I had the impression they had private reservations about Ranald as well as about my mother, regarding them both as disreputable, if for different reasons.

"She'll be back inside in a minute," said Mum, "mopping the kitchen floor to get rid of all our crumbs."

As we came to the dry creek she asked Jenny to pull over and stop the car.

"This is where the old dump was," she said.

I followed her around as she poked in the rubbish with a stick. It was slim pickings, but she unearthed a few old medicine bottles made of coloured glass and a couple of blue-and-white fragments of china encrusted in dirt.

"There were Chinese market gardeners here when I was small," she told me, "and one or two Chinese cooks."

More ghosts, I thought, more apparitions floating into the picture, then vanishing again. This time they had left a faint trail, a few shards of a rice bowl, a piece of a picture painted on a plate, depicting a tiny boat on a lake and part of a bridge.

Back in the car, she repeated the oft-told story of the Chinese cook my grandmother had sacked just after she first moved to Beaconsfield as a new bride.

"The cook had been working here for years," she said, "with all the men, when the house was just a shed and the kitchen was a lean-to on the side. She caught him dropping cigarette ash into the stew and told him he could pack his things and go."

"No me go, Missy," Jenny intervened, delivering the familiar punch line. "You go."

They both laughed at the thought of their eighteen-year-old mother trying to exert her non-existent authority over the staff, although I sensed an underlying sadness to this story, too. Jenny knew what it was like to be the sole woman in a household of men. No matter how kind they were—and my grandfather was by all accounts very kind—it must have been unspeakably lonely for my grandmother, and there must have been times when she was afraid. And what about the cook, lost out here, so far from anywhere he might have called home, his fate in the hands of a teenage girl.

We stopped again, just before the boundary gate of Beaconsfield, so that my mother could get out and fill one of her medicine bottles with soil. I watched her walk a few yards to where the dirt was fine and sandy. She went down on her haunches and scooped up a handful or two until she had enough.

Back in the car, she stuffed a tissue into the neck of the bottle to stop the dirt escaping. "A piece of home," she said.

o

Mum kept her bottle of Beaconsfield dust for many years and through many moves, until it was finally tossed out or lost, then forgotten along with everything else she had ever held dear. I don't know if she had any concept of home by the time she died. She talked obsessively about going there, begging me to take her home every time I saw her. But I wasn't sure where she meant. She had made so many homes by then, more than twenty. Some she had loved and some she hadn't. She certainly didn't mean the nursing home where she lived out her days.

"This is your home now," I'd tell her, trying to pacify her.

"Liar."

I wasn't with Mum when she died. Shin and I were living in Japan temporarily, trying to figure out a way for him to establish a base back in his home country. Before I left Brisbane, Sarah and I met up with a funeral director. We planned to arrange for Mum's funeral in advance, given that she was so frail. We felt a simple cremation was best, with a memorial service to be held later, at a time that suited the whole family. We didn't want anything religious because Mum had long ago given up on the church. Sarah suggested a party; Mum had always so loved a party.

"If we do it this way," my sister said, "you won't have to rush home if she dies. What would be the point? You've been grieving for her all these years anyway."

I was grateful to her for saying it, and for her sisterly concern.

What we didn't do was discuss our thoughts with Eliot. I can't say exactly why communications with our brother were so poor. The simplest answer is that we all lived separate lives in different cities—me in Brisbane, Sarah in Newcastle, and Eliot in the Blue Mountains, west of Sydney. The more complex explanation is that the fractured way we grew up had left us leery of each other. This was especially true after our parents' marriage started to fray. My sister and I could at least have a conversation, swap news on the phone about our kids, comfort each other about our mother's devastating decline, but my brother was much harder to talk to. I called him perhaps twice a year to update him on Mum's health. Apart from that, we never spoke.

According to Sarah, as Mum was dying, Eliot was the one she wanted to see, only Eliot. He came to sit with her, keeping a vigil at her bedside, holding her hand.

"He was very good," my sister said, "and very helpful when we had to clean up her room, get rid of all her stuff. But then he blew up."

"Why?"

"Because he thought it was selfish not to have a proper funeral. He thought we were just thinking about ourselves."

"Maybe he's right. Maybe we were."

For whatever reason, Eliot went ahead and arranged a funeral service in the chapel of the Catholic nursing home where Mum had spent the last miserable years of her life. Sarah didn't go.

"I never wanted to set foot in that place again," she said.

Given our lack of practice, it isn't surprising that my brother and sister and I failed so miserably to bury our mother's ashes properly. Up to this point I, for one, had never experienced the death of someone close to me. And we were, all three of us, without any religious belief, all of us clueless about standard rituals and rites. With no guidelines, Sarah and I were happy to improvise, but this did not suit Eliot, and he decided to act without us. Even to this day I wish he could have waited. At the same time, I understand why he didn't. If Sarah and I were acting selfishly, then so was he. We all were. We didn't know what else to do.

And so that's where things stood for a while. Eliot kept our mother's ashes with him in the Blue Mountains. The idea of a party-like memorial service faded away. I spent time in Japan thinking about other things. It wasn't until I returned to Brisbane a few months later that the question came up of where her ashes were to be permanently placed. I knew the answer. She wanted her remains to join those of her parents and grandparents in Brisbane's Toowong Cemetery. She wanted her name added to the others on the big pink granite plinth dedicated to the Murrays. She had taken me there some years beforehand to show me. We had packed a picnic and had sat on a nearby bench enjoying the spectacular view over the city.

"Bury me here," she said.

"Happily," I said.

At that stage I was still brushing off any premature death talk. Mum wasn't sick then, or not that I could tell. It's only now, looking back, that I think she suspected something was wrong, or else why start choosing burial sites?

About a year later, I rang my sister to suggest a plan.

"I was thinking we could all meet up in Sydney next weekend," I said, "have lunch together, drink a toast to Mum, then Eliot could hand over her ashes and I could bring them back here to do the deed."

"Where do you want to meet?"

"Chinatown. BBQ King. We could get one of the rooms upstairs. Mum loved that place."

"Who's going to call Eliot?" she said.

"I was hoping you might."

The fact is I was scared of my brother. He was too like my father for me to feel comfortable with him. I had been frightened of him ever since we were children together.

Sarah, being the oldest, was less easily awed.

"Chicken," she said.

Eliot arrived at the BBQ King a little later than the rest of us. Everyone was there: his son, Ben, then in his mid-twenties, who had been a favourite of my mother's, Shin and me and our two boys, Sarah, her daughter and two grandsons. Unfortunately Sarah's son wasn't with us because he wasn't speaking to his mother at the time.

"Mum adored him," I told my sister. "He should have been here."

"I tried," she said.

She stood up when Eliot came into the room and went around to kiss him. I preferred to remain seated. In his hand he had a large paper carry bag with Bulgari emblazoned on the side, which he placed on an empty seat.

"Is that her?" said Ben, peering inside. "What an ugly box."

He removed the box from the bag and placed it on the table. It was beige plastic, the size of a small shoebox, with Mum's name written on the front in marker pen.

"Put it back," said Eliot.

Ben did as he was told, carefully settling the bag back on the seat so it wouldn't fall.

"It's so small," said Sarah.

The talk went badly after that. There was a long argument about what we were going to order. It was the grandchildren who saved us from ourselves. Ben and the others regularly steered the conversation back to Mum, making sure the occasion was about her, and what she had meant to them growing up, and how they still missed her. And the great-grandchildren provided a useful distraction. There was always the topic of how they were doing in school, and what their favourite subjects were, and what they thought they might like to do when they grew up.

"Gamer," said the older one.

"Oh God," said his mother, her head in her hands.

After an hour or so there was nothing left to say. Everyone had trains to catch, or planes, in the case of Shin and me, and Eliot said he had another appointment somewhere else. In our rush to get away we almost forgot the ashes, sitting in the beige plastic box inside the Bulgari bag, until Ben remembered and went back for them. He handed them to my brother, who passed them to me.

"Thanks," I said.

"Nothing to thank me for," he said.

"It's what she wanted," I said.

"If you say so. I thought I might have taken them up to Beaconsfield and scattered them there."

"I thought of that too," I said. "But I don't think she belongs there."

"How would you know where she belongs?"

I couldn't think of a reply before my brother was out the door and down the stairs, leaving the question hanging in the air, unresolved. That was how it was with him and me. Every conversation was an argument, every encounter another chance to raise some point of disagreement, then leave before it could be settled. We were combatants before we were brother and sister. I was

ashamed for us. A different family might have managed
to put all of this history behind them and say goodbye
to their mother in style. As for us, all we could manage
was an hour of faked good fellowship followed by a hasty
retreat. I was glad Mum wasn't there to see it. She would
have been inconsolable.

Jenny was with me on the day, in 2010, when I in-
terred Mum's ashes. She drove to Brisbane from the Gold
Coast, where she and Ranald had retired to their holiday
house. Ranald was too sick to go anywhere by then; he
spent his days in an armchair in front of the television
with the volume turned up so loud Jenny had to leave the
house to get any respite.

"It sends me batty," she said. "He won't use earphones."

She was driving me up through Toowong cemetery
towards the Murray plinth. I had the beige box on my lap
and Jenny had brought a bunch of white lilies and a vase.

"Your mother always said, out of us three girls, she
was the lucky one," said Jenny. "We'd married men who
were tolerable, but she'd married one who was intolerable,
which gave her a reason to leave. I still think she was very
brave though."

"I don't think she felt brave," I said, remembering how
long it had taken Mum to end her marriage. Years and
years of conciliation and backtracking before she finally
made the decision.

"Does your father know she's dead?" said Jenny.

"Apparently he didn't quite take it in," I said, repeating what Ben had told me. By that time, I had become completely estranged from Dad. It was a consequence of so many things: the divorce, my father's mental instability since then, my desire to shield Shin and the boys from his worst excesses, and my illness. But Ben would sometimes go with Eliot to visit my father in his Sydney nursing home, and would subsequently relay news of Dad's condition to me. "He's very far gone."

"She told me she wanted to outlive him," said Jenny. "Even by a day."

"There's no God," I said.

o

I've never been to a Japanese funeral, but friends tell me there is a traditional ceremony after the body is cremated where the mourners pick through the ashes of the deceased with a special set of metal chopsticks. Bits of bone are lifted out for closer examination, signs are read, whether of fate or character I couldn't say, but apparently the ceremony can be funny—some of the comments about the dead raise a laugh, whether intentional or not. In any case, I imagine the ritual is helpful. I imagine the mourners derive comfort from this last act of intimacy with the person they have lost. I'm only sorry that I didn't think to do something similar before burying Mum's ashes, something to make the occasion more fitting.

As it was, Jenny and I stood by and watched while
two young council workers dug a hole at the corner of the
pink granite slab at the base of the Murray plinth. The
soil was rock-hard after weeks and weeks of dry weather,
but the workers chipped away until they had gone about
two feet down and about a foot across, just wide enough
to fit the beige box. I handed it to one of the workers, he
placed it in the hole, his colleague covered it with dirt and
tamped down the loose soil with the back of his shovel.
We thanked them and they left. And that was all. Jenny
and I said nothing, no prayer, nothing formal, only paus-
ing to arrange the lilies in their vase, before saying goodbye to Mum as if we were just leaving her for a moment,
to go down the road for a coffee. We didn't know what
else to do. When I think of it now, I wish I'd at least
thought to pour Mum's ashes into the hole so that they
could mingle with the dust, instead of leaving them in the
box. But I didn't, and I'm sorry.

I've only been back to visit the grave once since then,
after the stonemason finished carving Mum's inscription.
Her name was there: Everil Mary Taylor (nee Murray),
and her dates, 1921–2008, but I didn't sense that she was
there, and I wasn't tempted to talk to her or catch her up
with all my news. Actually, I had a powerful feeling that
she had long ago fled the scene and that the question of
where she belonged in death was still wide open. And I
realised that this was probably nothing more than the price

she'd had to pay for wandering so far from the place where she was born, that at some stage there was a point beyond which belonging was no longer an option. Her little medicine bottle full of dust was only an approximation of home, not the real thing, just like my burying her ashes was only a gesture at belonging, one that was bound to fail.

o

My father's name was Leslie Gordon Taylor, but everyone knew him as Gordon or L. G., and we children sometimes called him Captain Taylor. I never knew where he came from because he kept it a secret. Even Mum didn't know with any certainty. According to her, Dad's account of his past varied so often she could never be sure if, or when, he was telling the truth. It was known that he grew up somewhere in Sydney, but we were never taken to see his childhood house, or to meet his family, and his parents came to visit only rarely when I was growing up, certainly not often enough to leave any lasting impression. I cannot even recall now what they looked like.

If he talked about his boyhood at all it was to say how unhappy he'd been, cooped up in a little suburban box with a mother and father who didn't understand him, and no brothers and sisters to share his ordeal. He declared his father a bully and his mother a doormat, and told us he'd stormed out on them at the age of fifteen, never to return. He was vague about what happened next. There was a job as a jackaroo for some wealthy Victorian squatter, which ignited his love affair with horses, and where he might have picked up his patrician affectations—the cigar-smoking and the penchant for tailored clothes—although these could equally well have been acquired later, in the air force, where his character was truly forged, and where he grew his trademark handlebar moustache.

He was as hazy about his war as he was about his childhood. The air force to start with: it was obviously where his passion for flying began, and where his problem with authority emerged full-scale. He never said why he was thrown out, only that it probably saved his life, since so many of the other trainees had gone on to be blown to bits in the bombing raids over Germany. After that he simply got lucky, he said: one day he bumped into a recruiting officer for the British Army in India, who immediately convinced him to sign up for officer school. He duly shipped out to India for training. Six months later, his training complete, he expected to cross into Burma to fight the Japanese, but they surrendered before he could pack his jungle kit. I was never sure if he was pleased about this, or resentful, because it had deprived him of the chance to prove himself in combat. In any case, the end of the war saw him transported back to Australia anxious to launch his career in civil aviation as soon as possible, since flying was his true vocation.

Not that it was an easy calling. In the early days, when Dad was starting out, it was full of risks, all of which he seemed to relish. Along with travel. He couldn't stay in one place for longer than a year or two, or in the same job. He appeared to be in a perennial state of high dudgeon about the incompetent way airlines were run, about the primacy of commercial pressures over everything else. He fought with almost everyone he ever worked for. As a result, we lived like gypsies, forever packing up and moving on, which suited Dad perfectly. He was at his best when he was leaving. It didn't worry him if we had to change schools yet again, abandon friends and neighbours, repeatedly adapt to new surroundings. Anything, apparently, was better than settling down in some barren suburb like the one he'd escaped from as a teenager. That was Dad's nightmare, the thing he feared the most. I think he would have preferred to die than end up back in the same place he had started out.

He was in his seventies before he started to examine his beginnings with anything like equanimity. Growing up, he had always had a suspicion that, given how unsatisfactory they were, his mother and father were not his true parents. He remembered another couple, periodic visitors to the house, who came from Glasgow and bore an air of old-world refinement, people to whom his mother and father had deferred. In the hope, no doubt, of confirming his theory, he chose them as the first quarry in his genealogical hunt.

"They were called Auchincloss," my father told me. "There are five of them in the Glasgow phonebook. We've got to be related."

He travelled to Glasgow, where he discovered the truth. It was not what he had hoped. The couple were not his parents, but his father's relatives by marriage. And his father was not who he had said he was. Originally from Ireland, my grandfather had run away from a violent household at the age of fourteen or so, and ended up in Glasgow, where he changed his name from O'Neill to Taylor. An aunt took him in, and not long after that he joined the merchant navy and started travelling the world, eventually jumping ship in Sydney.

"I never knew any of it," my father said. "I might have had more respect for him if I had."

He showed me a tiny grey photograph of my grandfather scrubbing the deck of a ship.

"He was just a kid," he said, the first kind word I'd ever heard him say about his father.

My father spent a week in Glasgow meeting relations he never knew he had. He came back changed. It would be too much to say that he was at peace—he was never at peace—but there was some sense that he had laid a few ghosts to rest and decided not to run so hard. There was also some recognition of the price we had all paid for his insistence on always moving.

"It was tough on your mother," he said. "I don't blame her for quitting when she did."

He wrote to her asking for her forgiveness, but she didn't reply. By then, I am sure, all her reserves of compassion for Dad were exhausted.

My father's spiral into severe dementia probably started around the same time as my mother's. I should have recognised the signs, but I saw so little of him that it was hard to keep track. By then he was living in Canberra, where he had seen out his working life as a mail sorter for Australia Post, and now lived on a modest pension at a hostel for public servants. I went to see him there a couple of times, and Shin and I once visited with the boys on our way to the snow for a holiday. Now and again, he would turn up in Brisbane and knock on our door.

"Howdy," he'd say. "I was just in the area."

He'd proffer a shopping bag or two of groceries. "I didn't want these to rot in my room while I was away."

He gave the boys volumes from his library about planes and the history of aviation and was miffed when they didn't show proper appreciation.

"I'll take them back if you don't want them," he said.

As much as he enjoyed spending time with us all, he was really in Brisbane to see Mum. At that time she was living in an independent living unit a short walk from our house. Within minutes of his arrival he'd bring up her name.

"How's Ev getting on?" he'd say.

"Fine."

"She didn't reply to my last letter."

"That's probably because you asked her for money."

I knew this because my mother always showed me his letters, or read them aloud to me, her outrage mounting. It was twenty-five years since their divorce and my father was still trying to wangle money from my mother any way he could.

"He won't stop until I'm dead," she said. In one particularly cruel missive, however, he suggested she leave him her unit in her will, offering to pay half of any legal costs that might entail.

I now think this obsession with money was a sign of the deeper malaise that was about to engulf him. But at the time I saw it as nothing more than vengeance. He had not forgiven my mother for divorcing him. He resented her hard-won financial independence. He'd always scoffed at her job: school teaching was so drearily middle class. It had transformed her from the adventuress with whom he had fallen in love into a suburban frump. Going right back, it was clear that he was aggrieved my mother had family money and he didn't, even though, as my mother pointed out, it was her family money that had made all of his unfettered roaming possible.

"That's why he married me,' my mother told me. "I was his meal ticket."

The letters arrived more and more frequently, and were more and more upsetting for my mother. Not all of them were begging letters; some of them were newsy and contained cuttings he thought she might have missed from the paper. Some were long remorseful raves about their marriage and how it might yet be saved. But then along would come another demand for funds. "The twenty-five thousand that by my calculations you still owe me. After that I'll call it quits."

Foolishly, I decided to intervene. I called my father and told him to lay off. He didn't react well. There was some yelling down the phone, a lot of it insulting. Hearing him, I was transported back to my teenage years, when this sort of ranting had been commonplace. My heart raced as it had done back then, and I trembled all over. I could picture his face turning crimson with rage on the other end of the line, as he spat out his venomous barbs.

"You're a self-serving gold-digger who just wants the money for yourself," he said. "You see me as the competition."

When I couldn't listen to any more of his diatribe I hung up, hoping that would be the last of it.

It wasn't. Over the next few months my father wrote me a series of increasingly irrational letters. He was going to take me to court, he said, if I didn't allow him to see his grandsons, despite the fact that I'd never barred him from visiting and had no intention of doing so. But this was just a ruse: he liked to threaten people with the law. For years he'd been engaged in a fight with the Department of Transport over a decision regarding his pilot's license. He argued, with some justification, that a bureaucratic whim had ended his professional life. His "case," as he called it, had turned him into an amateur lawyer, with a lawyer's taste for combat. I didn't bother to reply to his letters, and eventually they stopped. Not so the missives to my mother. Every few months there'd be another letter. One day my mother simply stopped opening them and threw the envelopes straight into the bin with the other junk mail.

The last time I saw my father was at my brother's house in East Blaxland. Dad was not long out of a psychiatric clinic in Canberra, where he had been treated for depression. Against his doctor's advice, he had tried to wean himself off his anti-depressants; this had sent him into a black despair worse than anything he had experienced before. In the middle of the night he called Eliot to come and get him. My brother drove from the Blue Mountains through the night to Canberra and back again, then to work in the city the next day. After he called me, I rang my sister.

"We should go down," I said.

"No thanks."

I expected as much. Sarah's relationship with Dad was worse than mine, a history of mutual antagonism going back decades.

I flew to Sydney and caught the train to the Blue Mountains. Dad was waiting on the platform, unshaven and dishevelled, and relieved to see me. He embraced me affectionately, as if nothing untoward had ever happened between us. I had witnessed this often in the past. He could erase whole episodes from the record and pretend they had never taken place; whether this was calculated or genuine forgetfulness, I could never tell. It was particularly difficult now that his mind was in such disarray. After we had stopped at the butcher for some steaks, he led me home to Eliot's place, a neat little bungalow my brother had bought to be close to his ex-wife's place—and to Ben, who was then still a schoolboy. And for the next few hours Dad talked to me without pause.

It was nothing I hadn't heard before, a chronicle of woe I had seen played out in front of me for my entire life, the great drama of my father's rise and fall, to which all of us were witness whether we liked it or not. I am ashamed to say I didn't listen very intently. I was hungry and, apart from the steaks, there was no food in the house. I was cold and I didn't know how to work the heating. I was tired and

I didn't know where I was supposed to sleep that night, as both bedrooms were taken. Looking around my brother's kitchen, it struck me how lonely it must have been, when nobody else was there, and Ben was with his mother.

"Your brother saved my life," said Dad. "I'd be dead if it wasn't for him."

It was probably true. I knew my father owned a gun. Now he told me that, the month before he went into the psychiatric clinic, he had taken the gun to be cleaned and never picked it up again.

"I was afraid of what I might do with it," he said.

I could only stay one night. Shin needed me at home; at least that was what I told Dad. The truth was I wanted to get away as soon as possible, back to my boys. My father was out of danger. He was taking the proper dose of his medication and improving every day. When he wasn't talking, he was sleeping, so there wasn't a lot I could help with in a practical sense, and he was making an effort to shower now, so that was a good sign.

"How are you?" I asked my brother, once he arrived home from work, hoping to open up a conversation about his life. It was after dinner and Dad had gone to bed. My brother looked haggard from lack of sleep.

"Fine."

"Work okay?"

"Work's fine."

"Ben happy?"

"What's happy?" he said.

And there it ended, because it was too hard. We had never talked to each other about our lives before, so why even begin? But I can't help thinking now how much it might have helped us. We, Sarah and Eliot and I, had a problem. Both of our parents were ageing badly. Things were unlikely to improve for them, or for us. It would have been useful to hatch some kind of plan together, even if it was just a promise to keep in touch and talk things over, to keep each other's spirits up. But for some reason even that was beyond us. We seemed to be mired in the old familiar stalemate. Our default position was silence, but not of the harmonious kind. Silence for us was a form of accusation, an expression of mutual disappointment and rage, a substitute for violence.

My train wasn't until lunchtime. Dad and I had a sandwich at a cafe near the station. It was good to see that he hadn't lost his appetite. He talked and ate at the same time, dropping bits of food on the table and failing to notice, ordering more coffee than was good for him. He told me stories about some of the daredevil pilots he had known in his time, one or two who had died in spectacular crashes. He spoke of them wistfully, as if that was the ideal way to go. It was useless to try to interrupt his flow. I ate my sandwich, checked my watch, and wondered what all this talk really meant. It wasn't for me. I could have been anyone sitting there, a total stranger in fact, for all the interest he showed in my reactions. I assumed it was part of his illness, this utter disregard for the effect he had on others. But even at the best of times his self-absorption had been epic. His depression might well have worsened the problem, but I doubted it was the root cause.

"I better go," I told him.

"So soon?"

We crossed the road to the station, Dad still wearing the clothes he had slept in. We hugged on the platform. I brushed a few crumbs off the front of his sweater. He waved to me as my train pulled out, and that was the last I ever saw of him.

By the time he died, attitudes had hardened significantly on all sides. There had been the letters to Mum and the screaming down the phone to me, and there had been a showdown with my sister that had started out as a friendly chat and ended up as a shouting match. In the end, my brother had been the last man standing, the only one of us still in my father's good books, and the one he relied on for help. It couldn't have been easy for either of them. I knew all about dementia from watching my mother's disintegration. I can only imagine my brother was witness to the same degeneration in Dad, over about the same length of time, although Eliot never divulged as much. He didn't even call to tell me Dad was dead. I found out later, in 2010, from Jenny, who liked to call me once in a while to catch up on my news, and to tell me how much she missed Mum.

"I was so sorry to hear about Gordon," she said.

"Pardon?"

"He died."

"When?"

"Three months ago. You must have been away in Japan."

"Sarah would have told me."

"I heard from Murray."

Murray was my cousin. He and Eliot saw a bit of each other in Sydney. Ben had told me Murray and Eliot sometimes played tennis together.

I rang Sarah straightaway.

"Dad's dead," I said.

"You're kidding."

She was as incredulous as I was, not about Dad's death, which we had been anticipating, but about the fact that it had taken so long for us to find out.

There wasn't a funeral as far as I was aware. My only informant in these matters was Ben and he never mentioned any plans. But he did tell me, much later, what had happened to my father's ashes.

"Dad went horse riding in Mt. Kosciuszko National Park," he said, "and scattered the ashes there."

"Interesting choice," I said.

I was perplexed by the way Eliot handled things, made decisions on his own that, by rights, belonged to all of us. I know he had his reasons. I'm certain he thought that Sarah and I had abandoned our father, which in a sense we had, but only after years of provocation. The truth was that my father didn't really like us girls: we both knew it, and, over time, we both reached the conclusion that we didn't really like him either. I was also immensely sad, because here was yet another missed opportunity for my brother and sister and I to reach some kind of reconciliation after all the years of conflict and dispute, to finally bury all the acrimony of our parents' tempestuous marriage and make peace with each other. I pictured Eliot standing alone in the snow gums and pouring Dad out onto the ground at his feet, while his horse chomped greedily on the sweet alpine grass.

For a year or so, when I was in primary school, Dad flew supply planes for the Snowy Mountains Authority. He was based in Cooma, and lived there in a company barracks during the week. Every Friday night he drove to Canberra, where Mum had a job teaching in a high school. He seemed to enjoy the life, at least for a while. He said the barracks reminded him of air force life, and he liked the men he met on the job.

"Fascinating chaps," he told me. "From all over Europe. The mess is like a meeting of the United Nations."

He gave me a picture book about the dam the men were building and about the wonders of hydro-electricity. I studied it dutifully but without much comprehension.

I don't know why he left Cooma so soon. Perhaps it was the driving to and fro, perhaps it was the winter weather closing in. It could be foul up in the mountains, he said, and dangerous.

"You never know quite what you're heading into when you set out in the morning," he said. "It can turn so fast."

Perhaps it was just his perennial restlessness, coupled with an irresistible job offer to fly for Fiji Airways.

"It's a dream come true," he told us. "Chances like this don't come along too often."

And so we went to Fiji, at least three of us went. Eliot and Sarah were left behind in Sydney boarding schools, which they no doubt resented for the rest of their lives, as I would have, too, if it had happened to me.

If it had been my choice Dad's ashes would not have been scattered in the mountains. Apart from that one year, he never spent any time around Mt. Kosciuszko. It certainly wasn't home for him, any more than Ceduna was home, or Armidale, in New South Wales, where we lived for a while, or Suva, or Nairobi, or any of the other places we followed him to over the years. The truth was he didn't have a home. The closest he came to finding one was probably Glasgow, but by then it was far too late to make a difference. If it was a question of where he was happiest in his life, I'd guess it was in the cockpit of a plane flying somewhere over the Pacific Ocean. He loved to explain to me the meaning of the point of no return.

"If I'm flying between Nadi and, say, Port Vila," he told me, "I'm at the point of no return when I have enough fuel to reach Port Vila but not enough to get back to Nadi. In which case, I better hope I've read the charts right and Port Vila's where I think it is."

Talk of crisscrossing the Pacific energised Dad in a way that nothing else could. Life on the ground was a chore by comparison, something to be suffered until the time came to take off again. If it had been my choice I would probably have scattered Dad's ashes out of a light plane in mid-flight, somewhere out to sea, where they could have blown about in the wind currents for a while then sprinkled down over the waves. Who knows where he would have ended up then, in tiny bits and pieces spread anywhere and everywhere.

o

I'm not sure what I want done with my ashes. My problem is that, like Dad, I've spent my life moving around, so I'm not sure where to call home. In the past, whenever someone has asked me where I'm from, I've always struggled to answer.

"I was born in Queensland," I say. "But we left when I was a baby."

As if that means anything. Only that my mother came back to Queensland to have all her children, because my father was never home to look after her. I was actually born in a hospital in Southport, where Ril and Norman had a house they retreated to in the summer, and where all the families gathered for seaside holidays. Mum brought me back to the house after my birth and we were cared for by a nurse, which seems like an extravagance now, but these were boom years in the wool trade and such luxuries were apparently not unusual. I don't know where Dad was at the time, flying for the old Trans Australia Airlines I think, out of Sydney. Or perhaps he had already quit TAA and taken up the crop-dusting job based in Armidale. In any case, I have no memory of Southport, so it can't really count as home. I don't even know why I mention it when I'm asked, only that you have to start your story somewhere, and what happened next is too convoluted to bother with.

I should probably say I grew up in a car, crossing some interminable stretch of country, between a town I barely remembered, and a town I'd never heard of. It was the travelling that I recalled the best. Mum was usually at the wheel, Dad having gone ahead of us. In my memory, it was Mum who packed up all the houses, piled our belongings in the car, farmed out all the abandoned pets, then set off cheerfully down the road with hope in her heart that this might be the last time, the time we might finally settle and put down roots. But it was not to be, at least not for some years.

For a while, Canberra became home, not on the first try, not even on the second, but on the third, after a disastrous year spent in Kenya, where my father had a job flying for East African Airways. That's when Mum called it quits, when I was fifteen. In an act of sheer self-preservation, she dug her heels in and declared she'd had enough. She told me she was never going to move again. It turned out not to be true, of course, because Canberra was too small for the both of them once my parents had divorced. We did stay there long enough for me to finish school and university—only a few years, but it felt like an eternity to me. And I did develop a love of the place, not the city itself, which is stultifying, but of the rolling, empty landscape around it, and the broad skies above it. When I was old enough, I took my mother's car and drove all those wide, loopy roads leading out of town, just to see the country. Maybe that was me going home, back to those childhood voyages through days and nights of unfurling plains under their canopy of sky.

Nevertheless, I couldn't wait to get out of the place. When I left for England, I thought I was putting as much distance between me and home as possible. Over the next few years, I kept coming back to Australia—to see Mum, to make money—but escape continued to be my main aim in life, possibly my only aim. How else to explain the insouciance with which I got on a flight to Tokyo in 1982 with no real plan in mind, except to run away from Sydney, a city to which I'd decided I could never belong. Now I see it was only what my upbringing had trained me to do: pack up and move on, and never mind the consequences.

The consequences, in this instance, were only good. I've been travelling back and forth to Japan now for more than thirty years. Being married to Shin has meant learning as much as possible about where he is from, not just for my sake, but for the sake of our children. It hasn't been easy. Because we decided to educate the children in Australia I have not spent as much time in Japan as I would have wished, and I'm not as fluent in the language as I'd like to be. But what I have lacked in expertise I hope I have made up for in enthusiasm. There is a lot to love about Japan. If I have a home in that country it would have to be in Arita, the old porcelain town. There are dozens of places in Japan I would just as happily return to: Shirakawa, in Kyoto, where the spring cherry blossoms explode in a pink blizzard at the hint of a breeze; Yanaka, in Tokyo, where the megacity retreats and the old narrow streets are a warren of small-town traders and hip bars;

Mount Aso, where you can sit in an *onsen* outside and watch the snow fall on the cedars. In all of these places, and so many more, I have imagined I could happily end my days. If they are not my home, then they are places that have marked me, shaped my sensibilities, created affinities. Added together, they take up the space in my heart where my home would be, if I had one.

Shin and I have lived in Brisbane since 1998. Our sons grew up and went to school here. My mother died and is buried here. I'll die here myself. But Brisbane is not home to me. Not really. I'm a latecomer to this town. It still strikes me as an unlikely city, too raw and rough to take seriously. It does have its charms, however, and I do like the fact that on the streets of my neighbourhood I'm reminded all the time of my children when they were young, of my mother when she was still alive, of myself in a former life. So I'm attached to the place in that way, but not as attached as people I know who have lived here all their lives, and for whom the city is like a second skin. This is not the fault of Brisbane, it's just that there is a level of belonging I can never aspire to and must live without.

In Arita, where we have our other home, they make handsome porcelain funeral urns. I have asked Shin to decorate one for my ashes, with his trademark laughing skeletons, and told him to keep it with him until he is ready to toss me out. Where he should scatter me is still a topic for debate. We had always talked about going to Okinawa together, because it's a part of Japan we have never seen.

"Maybe take me there," I tell him. "You and the boys. You could find a pristine beach somewhere and throw me in the sea."

It's just one idea among many, and not very practical. None of us has the slightest connection to Okinawa, so the gesture would probably be meaningless, if not downright offensive to the Okinawans, who take their homeland very seriously.

Another idea we've had is to divide my ashes and throw half of them into the Brisbane River. Shin could then take the other half to Japan and scatter them in the stream that runs through the centre of Arita. What worries me is that Shin might well leave the town at some point, once he grows bored with it, and move to somewhere new, veteran nomad that he is. The best argument in favour of this plan is that it would satisfy a symbolic purpose, reflecting the way my life has been divided between Australia and Japan for three decades.

If I'm honest, I don't really care one way or another what becomes of me, so perhaps I'm not the right person to make the decision. The best thing might be for Shin and our sons to decide for themselves what to do. I'd prefer they make an arrangement that suits their needs and that brings them some comfort. I trust them to talk about it sensibly in a way that Sarah and Eliot and I could never discuss these matters. And I trust they'll be together on the day they dispose of my remains, so they can offer each other support. I'd urge them to go off to a bar together afterwards and grieve for me over a couple of drinks, because I know that's what I'd do, if I was in their situation.

III

ENDINGS AND BEGINNINGS

The photographer Hiroshi Sugimoto explains his obsession with the sea as stemming from an early childhood memory. He is travelling on a train with his parents. The track hugs the coastline, entering a series of short tunnels—light, dark, light, dark, light, dark—then emerges to reveal the bright sea stretched out in front of him all the way to the horizon. At that point, he claims, he comes into consciousness. This is me, here, now, seeing this—the sea, the sky, the sun.

Ever since I heard this story I've tried to remember my own moment of coming into consciousness. It's not my earliest memory—an insignificant recollection of playing in mud—but the time I saw a kookaburra swoop down from a branch to spear a skink and gobble it down live. This is what dragged me out of unconsciousness. This is me here, I thought, and that is you there, and where there was a skink there is nothing. Sugimoto also claims that immediately following his awakening to his existence he experienced a premonition of his death, and I'm prepared to believe him, because it was certainly that way for me.

The skink's disappearance was explicit. Things live until they die. Consciousness begins and then it ends.

How it ends I'm only now discovering. I can only speak for me, of course, and everyone is different, but dying slowly, as I'm doing, feels like a retreat from consciousness back to the oblivion that precedes it. This retreat is led by the body, which grows weaker and weaker, requiring less and less fuel and more and more rest, until a few trips to the bathroom and back are all the exertion you can manage in a day. I am no longer shocked by how feeble I am. My body is a dying animal. It is ugly and deformed, a burden I would like to lay down if only I could. But the body has its own schedule in the matter of dying, and its own methods, none of which I understand.

What I do know is that my world has contracted to the size of two rooms, my bedroom and my living room, because these are the rooms where I spend all my time. I sleep in my bedroom, I write and read and watch television in my living room. I'm much like an infant now, with an infant's dependence. My husband does all the shopping and cooking and takes care of all the chores. My son helps out with the driving, the banking, the running of the household, all of which I used to do when I was well. In the meantime, I lie around and dream. I most resemble a baby in the early mornings, when I first hear the birdsong outside my window. It takes me right back to the time of the kookaburra and my earliest lesson in death.

The more wakeful I become the more I yearn for the state of unknowing from which I emerged back then.

The kookaburra belonged to the first garden I remember, next to a eucalypt forest. The house was in a clearing but a few tall gums grew at the back and front, so that it seemed to me as if we were in the forest rather than separated from it. And the forest seemed to be in the house, because the rooms were full of forest smells and sounds, and because I brought the forest in with me from my games, and dreamed of it when I slept.

When I was on my own I played in the shadow of these giant trees, poking sticks around their roots to look for cicada skins, stabbing at the gobs of golden sap that oozed from the tree trunks, peering at the armies of ants that ran up the trunks towards the high branches. I stripped ragged lengths of bark and made houses for slaters and snails. When my brother and sister were home I went with them up into the bush, chasing after the dog. I regarded him as human, as human as I was, I thought, with the same feelings, the only difference being that I felt the cold and needed clothes. It fascinated me that he had eyes like mine, and a tongue the same colour, and feet divided into toes. I liked to watch his chest rise and fall while he slept. I liked to watch him eat dead things, and chase after birds, and shit in the forest. I even took to shitting in the forest myself, because it didn't seem strange to me after seeing him. Human, animal, it was all the same to me.

The point is that I never thought of my body at that time as something separate from the bodies of the dog, or the kookaburra, or the skink, or the mother cat up in my sister's sock drawer, who, one day, had somehow produced more bodies, tiny versions of herself. And I certainly didn't think of my body as separate from my new consciousness. They were one and the same thing, consciousness being a bodily sensation, just like sight, or touch, or hearing. So, if I had it, everything else must have it, too. I knew this, not from my reasoning, but because it was obvious. When a snail felt my touch, it curled up. When a bird saw me approach, it flew away. When I flipped my sister's tortoise onto its back, it righted itself and lumbered on. It was all only consciousness at work as far as I was concerned.

I enjoyed my body in the same way the animals enjoyed their bodies. I liked to lie in the warmth of the sun the same way the dog did. I liked my mother to clean my skin the same way the cat cleaned the skin of her tiny kittens. I loved to be fed the same way my sister's horse loved to be fed. For me, the kitchen was the centre of the house. The food my mother made in there was the greatest pleasure of my life, particularly the cakes—the taste of the batter on my finger, the smell of the oven as the cakes came out, the hot sweetness of the first bite. Or if I'd been sick and off my food, my mother would bring me a soft-boiled egg with toasted soldiers and the salty butteriness would take me to the epicentre of pleasure. I was still half convinced that my mother's body was made for this purpose, and for nothing else: to supply me with sustenance, to make me glow with health. And I did. I ran, I jumped, I swam at the beach, I learned to ride a bike and speed down the track at the side of the house. And I slept the deep sleep of the healthy and was undisturbed by forebodings or doubts. It was bliss to be alive.

As childhoods go, mine was remarkably free of upset. I never thought it strange that we moved around so much. It was just what we did. And it never cost me either my appetite for pleasure or my rude good health, so I was lucky in that way, and fortunate to have a mother who never gave me any cause to doubt her love. My father was the one to be wary of, but he was often away. Even when he was home, it was his indifference I had to contend with, rather than any outright antagonism. I'm talking about a time before his anger was ever directed at me. Back then he aimed his attacks mostly at my sister, and of course at my mother, who always bore the brunt of his discontent.

Dreamy would best describe me as a child. My early certainty that I was part of the animal kingdom resulted in a state of enchantment that stayed with me for years. No doubt this was in some part a defence mechanism, a way of insulating myself against my father's increasingly troublesome nature, but it had other advantages as well. It meant that for a long time I experienced the world as an unfolding series of glorious discoveries, as if everything in it was put there only for my enjoyment. I was drunk with sensation, in love with the unaccountable abundance and variety of things. Imagine my delight then when I found myself suddenly transported to Fiji, a place of such lush and uncommon beauty it made me reel.

For a child with my epicurean turn of mind, Fiji was as close to paradise as it is possible to get. Warm, sensual, full of smells and colours and sensations of extraordinary force. The light there was so pure it infused every object with an extra intensity, so that a flower was not just red, or a blade of grass just green, to be glanced at and then ignored. Flowers, grass, leaves, sky, sea, sand drew my gaze and made me stare, until I, too, was infused with red, green, blue, white, my body replete with brightness. For some weeks I lived in this state of dazed illumination, paying so much attention to light and colour that I became as entangled in them as I was in the beings of the dog and cat and the garden snails.

During this time we were lodged in a bungalow in the garden of the Grand Pacific Hotel, set back from the harbour front. This was my second garden, so different from my first. The trees here were nothing like the hefty eucalypts in the forest garden. These were slim coconut palms, some of them growing straight up, others leaning precariously into the ocean breeze, their fronds constantly clacking overhead. Men from the hotel would sometimes shimmy up them to reach the coconuts. I used to hear the fat fruit slamming into the ground like medicine balls, and I would stay and watch as the men slashed the outer skins away and cracked open the shells. I sat on the grass with them and chewed the white flesh they handed me. And I stared at their perfect limbs, and their strong teeth, and their gleaming hair, because I'd never seen bodies like theirs before; they seemed flawless. I was fascinated, too, by the way they moved, so easeful and languid, the women the same as the men. I never saw them hurry. Out of respect, I slowed down myself, lazed in fact, spending my days in a state of semi-wakefulness, either swimming, or lounging, or staring at the water where it lapped against the seawall. I was watching for snakes. The men had told me they were deadly, so I was drawn to them as a source of terror. The sight of one sliding through the oily harbour slick was enough to stop my heart.

At some point the subject of school arose. But in Fiji even school turned out to be a source of delight. I had been unimpressed with my first school, a charmless establishment for infants through to Grade Three, with draughty classrooms and asphalt playgrounds that bruised your knees when you fell. There I'd been clothed in a scratchy grey tunic that seemed always to be damp, and a bulky grey jumper if it was cold. I thought the outfit an insult to the body inside it. Perhaps this was because I associated the uniform with the humiliations I suffered while wearing it, the playground squabbles that left me bleeding from the nose, my demotion from Grade One because I was weak at sums. Others suffered, too, sometimes worse than I did, like the boy from our street who shat in his pants on the way home from the bus stop, in full view of everyone, and walked home with the offending material running down his legs.

Those kinds of accidents happened frequently at that school; it was a time of considerable bodily anxiety. My one pleasant memory is of a teacher running cool water over my wrists under a tap. I must have been out playing in the heat. She showed me where the veins ran close to my skin. "Your blood runs all through your body," she said. "So if you cool your blood down, that helps to cool the rest of you." It was the most important lesson any teacher had taught me thus far, and I loved her for it. I was immediately conscious of the blood pulsing in every part of me, and it was true that the cold water was drawing all the heat out of it.

To dress for my Fijian school I first needed to be measured by a tailor. My mother took me to downtown Suva, always a treat: the sights and smells of the narrow streets were captivating. The market in particular lured you in with its promise of plenitude. Here was a sweet-smelling maze of fruit stalls and fishmongers and farmers' stands selling things I didn't know the names of and had never tasted. My mother took notes for the time when we moved into a house with a kitchen and a house girl who could teach her what to buy and how to cook it.

"What fun this is!" she said, rubbing her hands together. I'd never seen her so excited. Perhaps it was because she'd made a new friend that morning in the hotel lobby.

"He's asked us both to dinner," she told me. We were drinking milkshakes during a break from our shopping. "His treat."

My father was away flying at the time, which always improved my mother's mood. She lit up when he was gone. Her skin seemed to glow and her eyes shone more brightly.

At the tailor's shop she showed me all the colours I was allowed to wear to school. On any given day I could choose between a tunic that was pink, mint-green, baby-blue or yellow. The tailor was an Indian, small, with coal-black eyes and stained teeth. He took my measurements, then pulled down a bolt of cloth so I could feel its weight and texture. I thrilled to the whole procedure, and understood that this new school must be an entirely different sort of place from the one I'd left behind. For a start my uniforms were to be made from this lightweight, open-weave cotton with its delicious sugary smell. While I inspected buttons and belt buckles and socks, the tailor turned his attention to my mother, persuading her to buy some blouses and a dress, exchanging banter and smiles with her as if they were old friends.

"What a salesman," she said, when we were finally back out on the street. "I couldn't say no."

Before we left town we stopped at a stationer's shop to buy my new schoolbooks. Stationery had been one of my earliest glorious discoveries. I had loved it since I could remember. I was a particular fan of coloured pencils in box sets or tins. There was a Derwent seventy-two collection that had reduced me to tears, probably because my mother had refused to buy it for me. But everything else appealed too, all the paraphernalia that went with making marks on paper: fresh exercise books full of lined pages just waiting to be filled, botany books with one page lined and one page blank, project books with blank pages throughout, sketchbooks for drawing, rulers, paste, scissors, fountain pens, nibs, ink, lead pencils, erasers. They were best when new, of course, when everything lay ahead of them, and before any mistakes and erasures had occurred. Which is no doubt why I loved them, because they were promise made manifest.

On my first day in class, I was allocated a magnificent desk. Made of solid timber, its hinged lid opened up to reveal a spacious cavity, where all of my stationery could be arranged. It was a more serious piece of furniture than I was used to, and implied a more orderly approach to schoolwork than I had so far experienced. As it turned out, orderliness was what I had needed all along, the sort of quiet, steady progression through things, which builds understanding and confidence. Our classroom was on the first floor, an airy, light-filled space that looked out onto mango trees and sports fields, and caught the sea breezes coming in off the ocean. I remember sitting there, watching our teacher shape the letters of the alphabet in cursive script for us to copy from the board, and sensing a shift in my consciousness almost as powerful as my earlier awakening in the garden. It had to do with the act of writing, which suddenly seemed like the most important thing in the world to practise and master, not for its meaning—that would come later—but for its mystery.

At first my devotion to handwriting derived from the pleasure I took in forming the shapes on the page, but along with that came something else, a yearning to capture things—sounds, speech, what I saw out the window, what I felt when it rained, what the villages looked like along the bus route to school—and make them communicable to others. The letters of the alphabet had this power. If you learned to draw them well and order them in the right way, you could tell anybody anything you liked, make a picture for them out of words, make them see what you saw.

This was a major discovery for me, that out of my hand and eye could come marks and symbols with magical properties. It meant that my consciousness could express itself to the consciousness of others and, though I didn't fully comprehend that at the time, I did feel it in the classroom: the beginning of a quest, of a search for the miracle of mutual comprehension that I have pursued to this day. I still write so as not to feel alone in the world, but now I type. What is lost in the process is the hand-drawn aspect of the written word—some of the magic has faded, as it must do from all childhood pleasures. They begin and they end.

A hotel is nirvana for a hungry child, or so it seemed to me. There is food everywhere, available at every hour of the day and night. I ate whenever I felt like it; I simply gave the waiters or the barmen the number of our bunga-low. Soon enough I didn't even need to do that. Once in a while my father tried to curb my appetites, by banning soft drinks and desserts at dinner, and threatening me with unnamed consequences if I continued to frequent the pool kiosk. But when he was away and my mother was in charge, I reverted to old habits and ate whenever I was hungry, without any regard to the cost.

Perhaps that explains why I took so readily to my mother's new friend.

"Order anything on the menu," he told me, in his lovely rich man's voice.

My mother had told me he was in oil. "A Texan," she said, although this meant nothing to me.

All I saw was a man with laughing green eyes and a broad smile and a thatch of sandy hair growing grey at the temples.

"A sailor," my mother had said.

"On a ship?"

"On a yacht."

For three nights we ate with him, and for three nights he said the same thing.

"My treat. Anything on the menu." He meant it as a joke by then, the Grand Pacific menu being as modest as it was.

But it was no joke to me. Delighted, I ordered a Coke each night, and finished up with that height of extravagance, a banana split with chocolate sauce.

I could see my mother liked her friend as much as I did, but I suspected her reasons were different from mine. I would look at her sitting up eagerly at the table and feel a shift in her, like a turning of the tide. She was still excited. Her skin still glowed and her eyes still shone brightly, but now there was something else that I couldn't put a name to. She seemed to hum. I wondered if I was the only one who felt it, and then I looked at the Texan and saw that he must be aware of it too, because his eyes had stopped laughing and he was watching my mother in a new way.

I had never seen sex before. I don't mean the act, I mean the presence of desire. All of a sudden there it was, as plain as day. It was the same thing that made the house girls giggle when they stood around the kiosk teasing the barmen. It was why the high school girls went silent in front of the boys on the bus. It was why my sister had got into trouble at her Sydney boarding school for talking to boys at the train station. My father had had words with her on the phone.

"Why do you insist on behaving like a tart?" he said.

At the time, I thought he was referring to some kind of cake. Now I wondered if my mother was behaving like a tart, too. I didn't think so. All she was doing was enjoying herself. It didn't last long. It was only a flirtation. Her new friend sailed away, my father came home, and that was the end of it. Nevertheless, I did start to watch her and my father more closely after that. Once desire had entered my sights, I started to notice it everywhere, even in my parents, who seemed more vulnerable the closer I looked, susceptible in ways I'd never suspected before, and not in full control of their faculties. Even their bodies appeared ready to betray them at any moment.

When my sister and brother arrived for the holidays, I saw the same vulnerabilities and susceptibilities in them and put it down to the same cause. Eliot had grown a foot taller, his voice had dropped an octave, he locked the door when he had a shower. In my sister the changes were even more pronounced. She had bigger breasts. She wore more make-up. Her skirts were so tiny you could see her underwear.

"You can't go to dinner looking like that," my father told her.

"Why not?"

"Because it's disgusting."

The boys in the hotel band didn't find it disgusting. They invited her to watch them rehearse. By the end of the week the lead singer was holding her hand and asking her to meet him after the show. My brother and I took to spying on them in the garden, watching them kiss and fondle each other in the hibiscus bushes. I don't know what my brother was thinking, but I always prayed they'd stop soon and say goodnight, because I knew my sister was playing a dangerous game.

It wasn't only the desire between her and the singer that was dangerous, it was the fact that the singer was black. You couldn't live in a hotel like the Grand Pacific and not know about race. It was the whole point of the place. The guests in the hotel were white. The hotel workers were black. One group was there to serve the other. That was the pact we had all entered into. Now here was my sister flouting the rules in the most flagrant way, allowing desire to challenge the order. My brother was the one who betrayed her. She was punished for her crime and returned to boarding school under a thunderous cloud. I wondered what the other staff had made of it all; they must have seen the way the singer had looked at my sister, and the way she had looked back at him. I'd seen it too. I was relieved when she finally went back to school and I didn't have to fear for her anymore.

As for me, even though I had become aware of the presence of sexual desire in others, I was not afflicted with it myself. I was so ignorant about sex that, when a kitchen boy took me into the deserted dining room one afternoon, I thought he was playing a game. We lay on the carpet, under a table, and he rubbed his hard body against mine for a few minutes while I waited for the game to start. And then it was over and we left. We even stopped in the kitchen to chat with one of the cooks about what he was making for dinner. He was chopping up fresh pineapples at the time and gave me a bowl full of dripping fruit to take outside. While the kitchen boy went back to work I took my pineapple and ate it on a bench by the seawall. As usual I looked for poisonous snakes in the water, waiting for the telltale flash of black and white. And there it was, unmistakable, a whip thin body, an arrow-like head, aiming for the deeper water further out.

As time went on, the workings of race revealed themselves to me in other ways that were less to do with sex and more to do with power. My mother found us a cottage in an all-white neighbourhood outside Suva. The only Fijians to be found were the gardeners and the housemaids who came out to work there. For a few hours every day, our housemaid would be busy washing our clothes in a copper in the back yard, sweeping the floors, making our beds and scrubbing the shower. And sometimes she would cook. Her specialty was a fish stew made with coconut milk and cassava. It would be waiting on the stove for my mother when she returned from the convent school where she'd found a job. I would come home from school to the sweet smell of the stew filling the house. It became as much a part of my life as the green mangoes and spicy dahl in greasy paper cones that we purchased from an Indian roadside stall a short bike ride from the house.

Of the housemaid's other life, her real life, I knew nothing, until one day she asked me to come with her to meet her family. It was a long walk in the heat. By the time we got there, I was sorry I'd come. There was nothing to see, just a concrete hut stained red from the surrounding mud, with an opening at the front and a couple of wooden flaps for windows. It was surrounded by banana trees and vegetable plots dug into the clumpy soil. In the doorway stood an older woman, perhaps her mother, and a clutch of children, all too shy to speak. I didn't know their names or their ages or even if they all belonged to the housemaid. And I didn't know how to talk to them. Perhaps I was shocked by the simple way they lived. Perhaps I was struck dumb by a nascent form of shame. I wouldn't, at the time, have been able to say exactly what I was ashamed of, but I did know that I wanted to get away as quickly as possible. I only had to look at the housemaid, for whom I had developed a sort of love, to see that I had disappointed her, and that the whole visit had been a mistake.

The discovery of my privilege was not glorious in any way, nor did it fill me with any pleasure. But it did make me see things that I might have missed before. It made me see, for example, how some girls took their privilege to be a right of birth and were not at all ashamed of it. My father had decided to buy me a bargain pony and join me up at the local pony club. I don't know why I agreed, when I wasn't a keen rider. I can only think I did it to please Dad, since horses were one of his passions. It was clear from the outset that I was outclassed. I knew some of the other girls from school, who had been riding since they could walk, in gymkhanas, competing for ribbons, all of which I knew nothing about. I didn't even really know the basics, so had to start out in a beginners' class, practising mounting and walking, while the other girls were taking their ponies over the jumps in the main ring. Perhaps my pony sensed my humiliation and decided to exploit it, because no matter how hard I tried I couldn't get him to obey me.

"You have to let him know you're the boss," my father advised.

"But I'm not," I said. "That's the problem."

I tried to imitate my friends, thinking I might fool my pony by faking a confidence I didn't feel, but he continued to take the same liberties, and I continued to flounder.

I don't think the other girls meant to be unkind, but they started to comment on my lack of general competency as a horsewoman. It happened in the stables as we were saddling up, or after the day's lessons were over. I would be brushing my pony's coat, or combing his mane, when they would start to instruct me in the proper way to brush or comb, in the right way to walk around a horse and the best way to handle a horse's hooves. I was grateful, but I was also aware of the pleasure these girls took in being my superior in all things horse-related. Their manner towards me was much the same as their manner towards the Indian man who ran the stables. They spoke to him in the same half-friendly, half-hectoring way, even though he was the same age as their fathers. I wonder that he didn't slap them, but he couldn't of course. They were protected by some invisible force field that shielded them from censure. Everyone could feel it, even me. So I thanked them for their advice and did as I was told. Not long afterwards I decided to quit riding altogether.

"I don't fit in there," I told my father.

And that was the truth. The pony club was not my world. I had wandered into something I didn't understand. My horse knew it even before I did.

If I tell these little histories now, it is because they conjure a feeling of what it was like to be me back then, the same but different, the body still growing up and out into the world instead of contracting and retreating from it. It's often said that life is short. But life is also simultaneous, all of our experiences existing in time together, in the flesh. For what are we, if not a body taking a mind for a walk, just to see what's there? And, in the end, where do we get to, if not back to a beginning that we've never really left behind? Time present and time past / Are both perhaps present in time future / And time future contained in time past. It is all, according to T. S. Eliot, the same thing. I am a girl and I am a dying woman. My body is my journey, the truest record of all I have done and seen, the site of all my joys and heartbreaks, of all my misapprehensions and blinding insights. If I feel the need to relive the journey it is all there written in runes on my body. Even my cells remember it, all that sunshine I bathed in as a child, too much as it turned out. In my beginning is my end.

The moments that stand out for me are the ones when I felt most alive. Even as a dreamy child, there were times when I came awake. Fear will do it, hence my fascination with sea snakes, and love, which in my experience is so close to fear there is barely a difference. "Every love story is a potential grief story," says Julian Barnes in *Levels of Life*, which is something I knew from a very young age.

I think most children do. It comes in the wake of consciousness. Everything lives until it dies, including the people we love the most, which, in the days of my dreamy childhood, was my mother. I took a trip with her around the main island of Fiji. We travelled with a girl I knew from school and her mother, my mother's closest friend there. We stayed at beachside motels along the way, driving from village to village, town to town, without any particular destination. At the end of every day there was always a beach and a swim and a bed with clean sheets, and no hint of disturbance.

Except for one evening. My mother took me out for a reef walk, to the very edge, where the reef drops away and the water changes from turquoise green to blue-black. The surf out there was pounding, the wind was blustery, and I wanted us to turn around and go home. But my mother stood firm, a wild grin on her face, her hair whipping around her head, her arms outstretched.

"Just look where we are!" she shouted, spinning around to take in the sweep of the beach behind us. I realised then how far we had walked, how tiny we must look from the land, two dots against the horizon. And I felt a surge of love for my mother, as if at any moment I might lose her to a rogue wave or a shallow swimming shark, for I knew they were out there cruising in the black water, just metres away.

"The sun's going down," I said.

"Time to go."

And so we made our way in, the tide rising around our feet and the sky turning mauve then orange then molten yellow.

That night I went over the scene in my head many times before I fell asleep, trying to settle my heart, but every time I pictured my mother's tiny figure surrounded by all that water I panicked again and my blood pounded. Even my sleep was filled with anxious dreams, where my mother and I were falling off the reef's edge into fathoms of churning water, and where it was up to me to save her. And then I would wake up and hear the surf in the distance and realise, with the most overwhelming sense of relief, that she was here with me, in the same room, breathing softly in her bed.

No wonder my mother and I remained close for most of my lifetime. We went through a lot together, when it was just the two of us. We even survived a Fiji hurricane, rushing around in our swimsuits to ready the house, while the rain came down in solid walls of water. My father was stuck on another island, so there was no one to help us. But my mother had her wits about her: she found where the hurricane shutters were stored under the house, and fetched a ladder. My job was to hand the shutters up to her one by one, which wasn't as easy as it sounds. They were heavy and the wind was careering around the garden in all directions at once. I had never seen such a display of force. It was animal-like in its ferocity, as if a herd of enraged beasts had been loosed upon us.

The cacophony continued all day and all night. We curled up together in bed and waited it out. There was nothing else to do but cling to each other for courage and warmth. The worst thing was the noise, the banging on the tin roof as the wind threatened to rip it off, the din of the hammering rain, the crack and clatter of the trees outside the window. There was no possibility of sleep. We lay awake and afraid; it was all I could do not to sob aloud for pity at us being so helpless. But I took my mother's lead and refused to give in to terror. By the morning, the wind and rain had started to ease off. It must have been two or three days later that we drove into town. It was a shocking sight. There was debris strewn everywhere, the road was full of potholes where the tar had washed away, trees were snapped in half. We parked by the harbour front, near a park, where two enormous shade trees had been upended. Their roots hung in the air, caked with mud, and people gathered round to stare as if it were a crime scene. I think sorrow was their chief emotion. I felt it myself when I came over to look. I took hold of my mother's hand and tried to communicate my love for her that way, because words seemed inadequate.

"Let's go and see what food we can find," she said. "We'll feel better once we've eaten."

○

I still miss my mother, even now. When I was told I had a tumour in my brain I was given a choice. I could have surgery immediately to remove it, or I could have a few doses of radiation to kill it off. Both methods were effective but each entailed an attendant risk. I didn't decide straightaway. I slept on it over the weekend. I was high on steroids at the time, and I remember lying in my bed, unable to sleep, silently discussing my options with Mum as if she could hear what I was thinking. I even asked her to pray for me, since I didn't know how to pray for myself. I thought back to how she had made it through some of the bad times in her life, and I recalled her reading her old leather bound Book of Psalms, a relic from her Anglican childhood. I couldn't even remember the Lord's Prayer from my days at Sunday school, though I did try. The Lord is my shepherd I told myself, and then stalled, thinking that, if only Mum was with me, she would know what to do, just as she had known what to do in the hurricane.

In the end, I opted for the operation, half hoping I wouldn't wake up at the end of it. You would know what that feels like, Mum, I thought, given how you died. How many nights must you have lain awake, praying that the Lord would take you in the night. If I should die before I wake / I pray the Lord my soul to take. But he showed you no mercy, and he is unlikely to show any to me. This was the tenor of my silent nighttime ravings. I was a child again, a little feverish and confused, unable to tell the difference between real and phantom, fact and fiction, and I wanted a cool hand on my forehead, a boiled egg with buttered soldiers, any sign at all that I was not abandoned.

Probably the lowest point in my mother's life was the year we spent in Africa. My father took a job flying for East African Airways, and my mother and I followed him. We left Sarah behind at teacher's college and Eliot in his first year of a cadetship at the ABC. It would be another adventure, Dad told us, and my mother must have believed him. Either that, or she was unable to deny him this last roll of the dice. Dad was getting on by then. Younger pilots were coming through the ranks and work was getting harder to find, especially the old-school style of flying that Dad favoured.

I didn't mind. I was in high school by then, and bored witless. Canberra felt like a desert to me, so devoid of life, you wondered some days if half the population had died in the night. I figured anywhere must be better. And Nairobi was better in many ways, at least for me. I went to a better school, I made brighter friends, I stopped hiding my love of learning. But in other ways it was a backward step. My father was unhappy almost from the start. In what was by now a familiar scenario, he started out with high hopes.

"This is the dream job," he said, puffing on a celebratory cigar. "The planes are the planes I love to fly, the routes are challenging, I get paid to travel. What's not to like?"

And then everything started to unravel. I never knew exactly why, although inept management was often mentioned as the chief culprit. It seemed as if the politics of race complicated everything: were the white pilots ever going to train black Africans to fly planes, if that meant putting themselves out of a job?

"It's mayhem," my father said. "There are fist fights in the cockpit."

His mood deteriorated rapidly. His temper flared. Home became a battleground, not that it was much of a home to begin with—a little, grey stone pile built to resemble a castle gatehouse. I helped Mum lock us in there each night, with our rented furniture and our handful of plates and saucepans, and hoped the thieves would leave us alone, because according to the neighbours they were everywhere.

To be honest, I feared Dad more than I feared the robbers. He appeared to be spinning out of control. He would go away for a couple of days and come back exhausted, irascible, liable to strike out at the slightest provocation. Sometimes he would be sulking at home for a week at a time, which seemed odd to Mum.

"Are you in any trouble?" she said.

"Nothing I can't handle, thank you very much."

Mum suggested to him that he quit his job and take us home.

"That's so typical of you," he said. "Cut and run."

"But you're so unhappy."

"What you mean is that you're unhappy." He made it sound like a criminal offence.

At night I would hear him shouting at her, trotting out all the old accusations. He had a list of grievances against her that went back to the day they were married, or so it seemed to me.

"I'm sorry I ever met you," he told her. "It's been downhill ever since."

"Perhaps we should end it then."

"What do you mean, end it?"

"Divorce," said Mum. "If that's what you want."

I knew then that things had hit rock bottom. Divorce wasn't something my mother had ever talked about. This was before it became common, when divorced women still seemed lewd and disreputable. And Mum had yet to read that electrifying call to arms, *The Female Eunuch*.

"Don't be ridiculous," said my father.

Eventually my mother could take no more.

"We're going," she told my father. "You come later when you've sorted things out here."

He took us on a farewell trip to the safari park outside Nairobi. We drove around for a few hours spotting giraffes and zebras. A troop of baboons held us up, demanding food, climbing onto the bonnet and staring us down through the windscreen, until they grew bored and loped away, casting contemptuous backward glances. As we returned to the park's entrance we stopped to walk around the enclosures where they kept injured or sick animals. I'd never seen a rhinoceros at close quarters before. I stood staring at the animal's enormous bulk, impressed by how harmless it appeared, for a creature so heavily armoured.

"Don't be fooled," said my father. "You're seeing him on a good day."

He might have been talking about himself.

He was on his best behaviour after that, helping Mum to pack and make arrangements, checking that all our flight connections were confirmed. At the airport he turned sentimental.

"So it won't be the Three Musketeers anymore," he said, hugging first Mum and then me. "All for one and one for all."

"You don't have to stay," said Mum.

"I was thinking I might go to England after I finish up here," he said. "See if I can find something there."

"Well, you always know where to find me."

Dry-eyed, she kissed him on the cheek and picked up her bags to go.

"I'll write," I said, suddenly feeling sorry for him. He had brought so much trouble down on his head for so many years. He looked broken, bowed, worn out. His eyes were full of tears.

"I should bloody well hope so."

It was a long flight home. The first stop was Karachi, where we had a lengthy wait, and the second Bangkok, where we arrived in a state beyond exhaustion, to discover that our Qantas connection to Sydney had not been booked and we were not on the flight. I'd never seen Mum in such a state of rage. She demanded to speak to the Qantas supervisor. When he arrived, all teeth and smiles, she launched into a history of Qantas, how her father had been a founding investor, how her uncle Frank had been the company's first booking agent in Longreach.

"Look him up," she said. "Frank Cory. Stock and station agent and editor of the *Longreach Leader*."

The Qantas man listened with feigned interest, then took our tickets and passports and scurried away to see what favours he could call in.

"I'm begging you," Mum called after his retreating figure. She didn't care who heard. "We have tickets, for Christ's sake. We paid thousands for them."

"You're shouting," I told her.

"I don't care. We have to get home."

She was right. We did have to get home. Not getting home was inconceivable.

An hour later, the supervisor reappeared and gave us the thumbs up. My mother fell at his feet.

"You're my saviour," she said, laughing and crying at the same time.

On the plane, she recovered enough to waylay a steward and order champagne.

"We'll be serving complimentary drinks straight after takeoff," he told her in his Australian twang.

My mother gazed at his boyish bronzed mask of a face. "Would you just say that again," she said.

He did as she asked.

"Thank you."

She turned to me and smiled. "We made it," she said.

o

Mum changed after that. Something had been resolved. There would be no more uprootings, no more abrupt departures. She had reached the end of the line. Now all she wanted to do was settle down. She counted herself lucky to still have her teaching job and her house. She too was getting older, starting to see her options shrinking, beginning to regret how much she'd squandered in her efforts to placate my father for so many years.

He came home, of course, as she knew he would—jobless, angry, spent—and notched up Africa as another grand adventure gone terribly wrong. He moved into the back room, the smallest room in the house, the one we called the guest room, while my mother stayed in the main bedroom and slept in the double bed alone. Back in Fiji, when I'd first seen what desire looks like, I had never imagined it could so easily mutate into its opposite, which in my parents' case was a sort of barely contained contempt. I had imagined desire to be unquenchable, but now I realised that it began and ended just like everything else.

My father's room was a tomb to desire. I used to go in there to deliver his folded washing and vacuum the floor. I suspect I took on these jobs to save my mother from doing them. I didn't think she would want to see the unmade bed, the dusty bookcase, the hairbrush, the comb, the nail clippers, the razor, the shirts and ties hanging forlornly in the wardrobe. For me the sight of Dad's scant belongings was melancholy enough, but for her it might have been close to unbearable.

"This can't go on," she told my father.

They were arguing again, about the usual things, after which my father refused to speak to Mum for a couple of days, except to ask for more sauce for his sausages, or more cream for his coffee.

"Get it yourself," I told him, tired of his surliness, so he refused to speak to me as well.

"What do you propose?" he said, deciding to confront her.

"A separation," said Mum. "I've spoken to a lawyer and I've been to the bank. I can borrow enough to buy you out."

This wasn't news to me. Mum had already told me her plans. But Dad could not have been more shocked if she had produced a gun and threatened to kill him.

'I don't believe you."

She went to the study and brought back the papers. As she laid them out in front of him her hands trembled violently.

"Take your time," she said.

It was two more years before he signed. Some of that time he spent in Indonesia flying political prisoners from Java to a prison island called Biak. But mostly he spent it at home idling, growing more and more despondent, more and more enraged that a man of his talents and ability could have sunk so low. What's more, none of it was his fault. Fate and circumstance had conspired against him, in league with his wife, who should have been his loyal helpmate, but instead had made it her mission in life to sabotage him.

"That's rubbish," she told him.

"You would say that."

He moved out one winter's day, taking just a couple of suitcases.

"I'll come back for the rest once I'm settled," he said.

"Where will you stay?" said Mum.

"What do you care?"

He was headed for Sydney, where he claimed to have some old friends.

"We'll keep your things in the garage," said Mum.

"That's big of you."

And then he drove away up the street with his fog lights on.

"Oh God," said Mum, "what have I done." It was a statement not a question. It meant she had just crossed a line that would stay crossed forever.

o

My mother's first love was a lawyer, killed in the war. He was on a reconnaissance flight over a beach somewhere in the Solomons when the plane slammed into a tree and crashed in a ball of flames. By sheer coincidence her brother Peter was on a ship not far off shore and saw the whole thing, but he didn't tell my mother that until years later. The truth was, my mother's parents were relieved when Mum's paramour was killed, because he was from Melbourne and half-Chinese and therefore unsavoury on two counts.

Growing up, I was haunted by this story. It might have turned out so differently. The lawyer might have come back from the war and married my mother. And they might have had children, who were not my sister, my brother, and me, but entirely different people. In which case, my sister and brother and I would not have existed, ever, anywhere. We would have been nothing. It was only because an accident intervened that we were here, the replacements, the lucky ones.

The accident of birth is just that. And so is everything that happens afterwards, or so it seems to me. How many times I could have died before now, and in how many different ways. And yet I came close only once: a speeding sedan ran a red light, hit three other vehicles, and jackknifed into my rear wheel a split second after I'd stepped out of my parked car. A bystander described the scene to me later.

"You were a millimetre away from losing your legs," he said.

I hadn't seen a thing, only turning as the sedan came to a halt and the teenage driver emerged unhurt.

"My brakes failed," he said, shaken and apologetic. "I couldn't stop."

So many times I've wondered what might have happened to me if I had lost my legs, or even just my right one, where my first melanoma appeared two or three years later. If I'd just been a second slower stepping away from the car, I might not be dying now. I'd be legless, of course, but still in good health. Of these fateful forks in the road are our lives made up. We are all just a millimetre away from death, all of the time, if only we knew it. The *Hagakure* is a samurai manifesto, written in 1716, to remind its readers of this incontrovertible fact. "It is silly," writes the book's author, Tsunetomo Yamamoto, "to spend an entire lifetime struggling and worrying and doing things we don't want to do; after all this life is like a dream, so short and fleeting." It's a good piece of advice even now.

And of course I wonder why I was not more vigilant about checking my skin, because, if I had been, I would have picked up that first melanoma before it turned bad, and saved myself a lot of heartache. When I was first diagnosed, I was angry with myself for being too lazy and stupid to bother with anything but the occasional quick examination. But then I decided that kind of thinking was a waste of my time, because we start dying the moment we are born. I know that now, not in the child's way I knew it when I saw the skink disappear down the kookaburra's gullet, but in a dying person's way. The knowledge has changed from that first illuminating but soon forgotten premonition into an undeniable lived reality.

I imagine at the very end I might feel a little like my mother felt when her marriage finally died. Oh God, what have I done. I've crossed the line. What started out so well, and seemed so full of promise, has come down to this, a big zero. But that presumes that I will be lucid to the last moment and able to think this final thought. If

I'm being realistic, that isn't the most likely scenario. As far as I can tell, I'll either succumb to some opportunistic infection, for which I've refused antibiotics in advance, or, having similarly declined forced feeding, I'll starve to death. Every day, my body demands less and less fuel and, although I still enjoy food, I eat like a bird, much to Shin's despair. He's always been the family cook. He's been feeding me since the day we met. Everything I know about Japanese food I know because of him. So now that's another pleasure gone, perhaps the greatest. I don't know how long it takes to die of starvation, or whether it hurts, but I dread it, just as I dread my sons watching me go like that. Because that will be what they remember, their mother reduced to a bag of bones. What it will do to Shin I can't bear to contemplate.

And all the while my Chinese drug offers an alternative way to go. I'm grateful to have it. It helps me to feel that my autonomy is still intact, that I might yet be able to influence my fate. Even if I never use the drug, it will still have served to banish the feeling of utter helplessness that threatens so often to overwhelm me. I have heard it said that modern dying means dying more, dying over longer periods, enduring more uncertainty, subjecting ourselves and our families to more disappointments and despair. As we are enabled to live longer, we are also condemned to die longer. In that case, it should come as no surprise that some of us seek out the means to bring a dignified end to the ordeal, while we are still capable of deciding matters for ourselves. Where is the crime in that? A sorrowful goodbye, a chance to kiss each beloved face for the last time before sleep descends, pain retreats, dread dissolves, and death is defeated by death itself.

I've come to the edge of words now, to the place where they falter and strain in the face of dying's terrifying finality. The reason I was always such a fan of film is that films are about showing not telling. If I were writing my death scene for a film my very last moments would go something like this. A montage. Shaky, over-exposed home-movie footage of a girl with a dog in dappled sunshine, a car speeding down a dusty road, the same girl on a beach with palm trees, arm in arm with her mother in some outback moonscape, crossing the tarmac at an airport with a silver jet in the background. The jet takes off. A kookaburra sits on a branch laughing. A skink slinks away under cover.

Fade to black.

ACKNOWLEDGMENTS

This book would not have happened without Penny Hueston, my editor at Text, who gave me the idea and cheered me along throughout. For all their love and kindness along the way I'd like to thank Yuriko Nagata, Terry Martin, Alfreda Stadlin, Peter Dodd, Kaoru Kikuchi, and John Slee. To Barbara Masel, who for so many years has been my first reader, my friend, my adviser, I owe too much to ever express or repay.

I'm also deeply indebted to the nurses and staff at Karuna, who have provided me with the peace of mind to work on this project despite my failing health. I could not have wished for more compassionate care and counselling over these past months. And my thanks to the late Susan Addison.

And of course I thank Shin, for everything he is and does.

CORY TAYLOR was born in Queensland in 1955. She was an award-winning novelist and screenwriter who also published short fiction and children's books. Her first novel, *Me and Mr. Booker*, won the Commonwealth Writers' Prize (Pacific Region) in 2012 and her second novel, *My Beautiful Enemy*, was short-listed for the Miles Franklin Award in 2014. She died on July 5, 2016, a couple of months after *Dying: A Memoir* was published in Australia.